"In this powerful book, Kevin Baum opens the back door to the fire house and invites his audience into the fellowship of firefighters. He shares his experiences as if around the firehouse table, reliving the exhilarating drama and emotion of his stories. It is hard to imagine a profession where quick decision-making and strong leadership are more necessary than that of fighting fires. The clear and thoughtful leadership principles demonstrated in this book have been forged pure by men and women who face life-threatening emergencies on a daily basis. These principles are as powerful in the office, the boardroom, or the operating table as they are on the line, fighting fires."

Michael Conlin, MD, FACS, Professor & Surgeon,
Oregon Health & Sciences University, Portland, Oregon

"Unlike many management books today, *Lessons* is a page-turner that will captivate you. Each chapter is flush with learning opportunities for community and business leaders, as well as for families and individuals. Readers of all ages will benefit from this insider's look at the fire service. *Lessons from the Line* will challenge every reader to examine what it takes to execute a vision effectively; whether leading a company, a classroom, a sports team, or a family, this book is a *must read*."

John C. Fleming, Former International CEO
President, Meridian Asset Management, Inc.
Austin, Texas

"*Lessons from the Line* is a fantastic book and a must-read for anyone seeking to become a true inspirational leader!"

Ben-Saba Hasan, Vice President, Dell, Inc.
Austin, Texas

"*Lessons from the Line* will do for the fire service of the twenty-first century what *Report from Engine Company 82* did for the fire service of the twentieth century, with the added bonus that Kevin skillfully creates a bridge from firefighting to universal leadership principles. The stories are nail-biters and the lessons are right on target. *Lessons* is a reading pleasure that provides leadership tools that will help not just managers, but anybody who wants to improve performance. Bravo, Chief Baum!"

Fire Chief Gary Aleshire,
Snohomish County Fire District One
Seattle, Washington

"This is a truly effective book about leadership and management principles that is also fun to read, uplifting, and irresistibly motivating! *Lessons from the Line* is destined to become a leadership classic—one you will refer to again and again for renewed inspiration and encouragement. By skillfully alternating heartfelt stories from his twenty-one years of experience as a firefighter with practical and understandable lessons about leadership, Kevin teaches us fundamental truths about both leadership *and* life. These are powerful prescriptions to cure whatever may ail you or any organization you work in or lead. As you read these always fascinating and sometimes heartbreaking stories and the lessons that follow, you will laugh and cry and also be powerfully energized to confront your own failures and fears and overcome them to achieve more than you ever thought possible."

Robert J. Stall Jr., JD
Chief Deputy Public Defender
San Diego, California

"*Lessons from the Line* demonstrates how one of the largest organizations in the world uses simple principles that drive consistency and excellence universally. These principles—the power of a clear mission, leveraging failure, taking risks—can have an enormous impact on any organization. Unfortunately, too many organizations today get lost on their voyage to excellence. I would encourage any business leader or manager of any organization to read this book as a tool to help them reset and rethink their current organizational reality."

Daniel Kube
Vice President World Wide Marketing & Alliances
Actuate Corporation
Toronto, Canada

LESSONS
FROM THE
LINE

LESSONS FROM THE LINE

WHY EVERY LEADER SHOULD BE A
FIREFIGHTER FOR A DAY

KEVIN BAUM

TATE PUBLISHING & *Enterprises*

Lessons from the Line
Copyright © 2007 by Kevin Baum. All rights reserved.

This title is also available as a Tate Out Loud product. Visit www.tatepublishing.com for more information.

No part of this publication may be reproduced, stored in a retrieval system or transmitted in any way by any means, electronic, mechanical, photocopy, recording or otherwise without the prior permission of the author except as provided by USA copyright law.

This book contains descriptions of situations and events that are recounted as accurately as possible from the author's memory. Some of the names of those involved have been changed in order to protect their privacy.

This book is designed to provide accurate and authoritative information with regard to the subject matter covered. This information is given with the understanding that neither the author nor Tate Publishing, LLC is engaged in rendering legal, professional advice. Since the details of your situation are fact dependent, you should additionally seek the services of a competent professional.

The opinions expressed by the author are not necessarily those of Tate Publishing, LLC.

Published by Tate Publishing & Enterprises, LLC
127 E. Trade Center Terrace | Mustang, Oklahoma 73064 USA
1.888.361.9473 | www.tatepublishing.com

Tate Publishing is committed to excellence in the publishing industry. The company reflects the philosophy established by the founders, based on Psalm 68:11,
"The Lord gave the word and great was the company of those who published it."

Book design copyright © 2007 by Tate Publishing, LLC. All rights reserved.
Cover design by Isaiah McKee
Interior design by Janae J. Glass
Edited by Brianne Webb

Published in the United States of America

ISBN: 978-1-60462-503-5
1. Self-Help: Personal Growth
 2. Business & Economics: Motivational/Management: General

07.11.06

To Jim Baum and Roy Bosson, two great leaders.

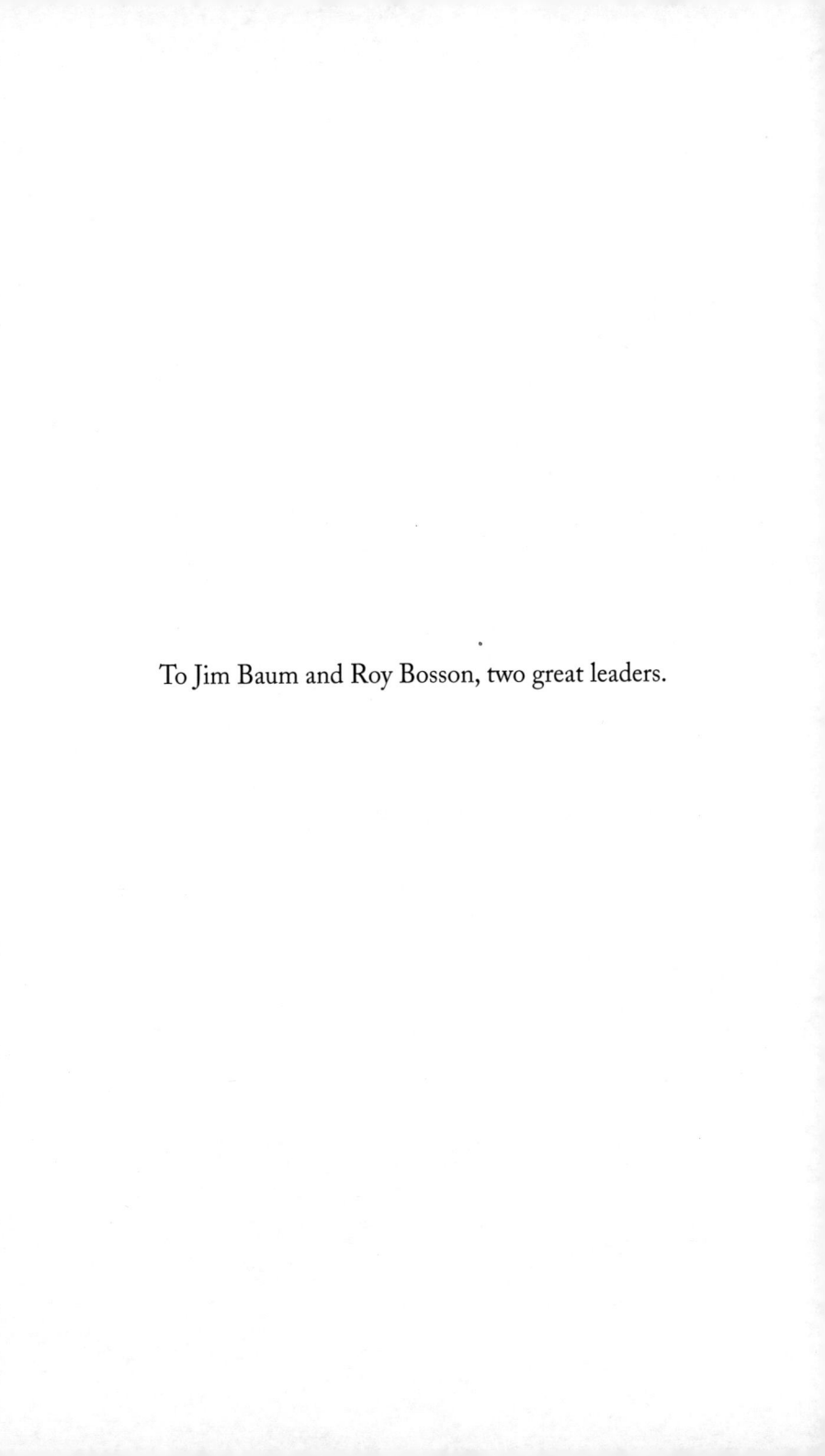

TABLE OF CONTENTS

13	Introduction
19	Prologue: Answering the Call
33	The Power of Purpose
53	Lesson: Mission Clarity
59	Dare to Care
77	Lesson: Service Commitment
87	Give up the Nozzle
117	Lesson: Structured Empowerment
125	Tradition Matters
151	Lesson: Community and Fellowship
159	Sleeping with Failure
189	Lesson: Organizational Learning
201	The Dragon Slayer in You
221	Lesson: Innovation and Renewal
229	Epilogue: The Firefighter Model in Review
235	Notes
245	Acknowledgements
247	Author's Note
251	About the Author

INTRODUCTION

Imagine a world where you can pick up the telephone, dial three simple numbers and instantly be connected to a human, make an urgent request for service, and in less than five minutes have millions of dollars of resources and dozens of experts arrive at your door with a simple question on their mind—"What can we do for you today?"

Sound absurd?

In fact, here's a fun exercise for you: Go to your computer and Google "Fortune 100 companies." Pick any three off the list, find their main phone number, look at your watch, and give them a call. Time how long it takes to actually speak to a human. I'll wager it takes more than five minutes. As you are all too aware, today our typical experience anytime we call a business is to spend an annoying amount of time on the phone going through automated voice menus and push-another-number frustrations, even when we are trying to *buy* a product or service. In fact, one major airline actually *charges* an additional fee if you want to talk to a human to complete an airfare transaction!

In today's world of Internet self-service, voice navigation systems and "I'm sorry, I will be out of the office until 2010" auto e-mail replies, it is becoming difficult to feel like we are anything more than simple consumer statistics in an increasingly impersonal world. Indeed, in our efforts to automate everything and to hold "economy" and "efficiency" as the continuous carrots of competitive positioning, I wonder if we have lost sight of why our organizations exist in the first place. So much of today's pursuit of profit and scale seem to place the organization first and the customer, well, last. What's particularly disturbing is that this trend of self-service, automated efficiencies appears to be on the rise— almost a self-feeding cycle of efficiency competing against efficiency until ultimately, I fear, we will all be sitting in our little home offices ordering everything we need for existence off the Internet. What a terribly antisocial thought!

There is hope. The scenario I presented in the first paragraph is actually possible; in fact, it happens *thousands of times a day*, every time somebody has an emergency. Think about it. When you pick up the phone and dial those three magic numbers, 9-1-1, odds are you are about to receive a visit from a host of complete strangers who all have one single-minded purpose driving them—*helping you.*

Is there any other business model on the planet where you can expect the same level of service? Find *one* Fortune 100 company that can make the same service commitment.

You can't. And you won't.

But you can find it at your local fire department.

Much has been written about the emergency services since September 11, 2001. The tragic events of that terrible day roused a public fascination for the emergency services in general and firefighters in particular. Most firefighters find this renewed interest in their occupation as a welcome embrace and validation that their efforts are valued and appreciated. Others find it to be mildly embarrassing and too much attention for a traditionally humble profession.

As a twenty-one-year veteran of the fire service and today as a consultant working on organizational development and performance, I find the public fascination for firefighters and their occupation to be a compelling invitation to explore, to drill deeply into the well of this occupation, and to ask some important questions: Why are firefighters so universally valued? What is it about their occupation and the nature of their service that makes them so appreciated? How can it be that a home can burn completely to the ground, and yet the owners still bring the responding firefighters milk and cookies, give them hugs, and tell them thank you? Are there any lessons for leaders or managers that can be extracted from this profession and applied to organizational life in general?

I think these questions are particularly important given the recent corporate trends to chase efficiencies at almost any cost (pun intended). Indeed, I think this conversation is *urgent*. Here's why: As organizations today busily occupy themselves with "flattening" the world, are we inadvertently flattening expectations of corporate services in the process, slowly creating a do-it-yourself society? Have we become unwitting accomplices to a cultural shift that puts the company and its profits ahead of the customers and their experience? If this is the case, what are the unforeseen consequences of this trend? Indeed, when is the last time you even considered giving a complete stranger a hug and a thank you for a service or product?

Where have all the heroes gone?

While much can be written about both good *and* bad leadership practices in the fire service, one truth does seem to hold constant—their customers love them. Imagine if you could capture and maintain the same loyalty from your customers. Imagine if you could capture the same loyalty from your employees. What would you stand to gain?

In this short book, I will be exploring what I call the "Firefighter Model." This name describes what I consider to be the synergy of a few leadership and management principles that seem to distinguish the fire service from other industries and to win them hugs from complete strangers and unwavering customer support. I have organized this conversation simply. Each chapter begins with a story from my own experience, and then ends with a few thoughts on important leadership lessons that can be extracted from the experience. The principles I discuss in this book aren't complex nor are they confused by an abundance of academic citations, but they don't have to be. These lessons are real, and every day they make a difference in how the fire service performs and is perceived by its customers. I think they are important lessons to share.

While both the title and the thesis of this book are geared toward organizational leaders and managers, the stories and lessons have universal application and appeal and can serve as stimulating seeds for personal improvement as well. I encourage anyone who is interested in self-renewal, personal growth, or leadership to take this short journey with me. After all, we are all leaders in one form or another, whether it's family, church, work, or life. We can all learn a great deal from the Firefighter Model and grow in the process.

Finally, this book reflects years of observation and experience, not to mention numerous sleepless nights ruminating on my many fire service experiences. I reflected on these experiences from many different perspectives—personal, organizational, management, leadership, and others—and have informed these experiences through years of academic and practical research into management and leadership practices. In fact, the more I reflect on the Firefighter Model, the more I become convinced that we can extract some powerful lessons from this unique profession—lessons that can have a profound impact on our own lives and organizations. I think you will find this conversation to be both interesting and valuable, and I hope you will be able to apply much of what I have learned from this journey to your own efforts to improve performance, whether it is personal performance or organizational.

PROLOGUE
ANSWERING THE CALL

I remember the day well. It was a typical June day in Austin, Texas: 95 degrees, 95% humidity, sweltering, and downright miserable. Live in Austin long enough and you learn to accept the sweat, the stained clothes, and the smell of bodies in various states of dehydration. You can always tell a newcomer to the area because they carry a handkerchief that they constantly pull out while they remove their glasses, dab their forehead, and remark on the oppressive heat. "It *is* hot in Texas!" The rest of us just carry bottled water, wipe the sweat with our sleeves, and call it cool. Austin is funky; so are the people and so is the weather.

It was my second month in the firehouse after completing the Austin Fire Department's six-month training academy, and a shift whose date I can't recall. The date really doesn't matter. Here's what I do remember: It was 1985, and I was twenty-two years old and full of grand notions of public service, civic duty, and fire-scene heroics. I considered myself a born firefighter and absolutely could not wait for my first emergency response of "significance."

Up to that point, the most significant incident I had experienced was a totally involved car fire, and I was only given nozzle time after the fire was out. My crewmate, the "senior" firefighter, put the fire out while I backed him on the line and the officer walked the perimeter. After the fire was out and the danger (and fun) had passed, he handed me the nozzle with a shrift comment: "Here, Rambo, play around for a while." I felt like a kid whose big brother just gave him the broken Tonka Tractor to play with. I was itching to see something incredible, get in harm's way, and be *on the line*. Here I was squirting water on a car fire that was already out and named Rambo for the effort. Of course the nickname stuck.

Being a rookie in a firehouse is the bottom of the food chain—literally. In fact, the first firefighter I met at Fire Station Six on my very first tour of duty was a woman named Jane. She met me at the back door, blocked my entrance, looked me up and down several times, and remarked, "Ahh, fresh meat. I love fresh meat, and you look tasty!" She turned on a heel and growled as she left. I stood there dumbstruck, frankly not knowing what I should say in reply. My hasty remark: "Thank you, sir!" Not an auspicious beginning.

Rookies are just the greenhorns that think they know what they are doing but don't, have lots of book smarts, and have no street experience. I kept reminding myself of this fact, as well as of the wisdom of the food chain I learned in the fire academy: earn your rights through passage, learn from those with experience, don't screw up, never forget the ice cream, shut up, and answer the phone.

On this particular shift, in addition to being the official answerer of the phone, I was also the designated "traveler." Traveling, in the fire service, simply means you are a virtual firefighter for a day—not assigned to any specific firehouse but available at large to fill in staffing gaps across the city. Interestingly, the tradition of traveling firefighters is almost as old as the profession itself. For as long as there have been fire stations, there have been staffing issues that require trained firefighters to move from one house to another to provide adequate response coverage. In fact, in the "old days," firefighters would simply meet at the beginning of a shift for roll call and daily station assignment. "Placement," in those days, was conditional depending on the demands of coverage. You had no station assignment, no office, no locker, and no crew. You belonged to the department and the citizens you protected, and you carried a duffle wherever you went.

Regardless, traveling can be a very frightening experience for a rookie. You're already surrounded by a bunch of people who you find intimidating and you really don't have a clue as to what you are doing. You have to sleep, eat, work, clean, shower, train, and respond to emergencies with a bunch of strangers. Not a cheery scenario, but one you have to accept if you want the job.

After a fair amount of wrangling to develop a staffing strategy for the battalion, my chief finally gave me an assignment for the shift—Fire Station Twenty in deep south Austin on a road called Manchaca. I remember asking for the address and how to pronounce the street and in reply got a wiseass answer from a firefighter nicknamed after a farm animal.

"Get your gear and get out of here, Rambo!" I scurried off eager to please, confident that I could find the station on my own and completely unaware that this tour of duty at Fire Station Twenty would in many ways change my life forever.

Twenty minutes later, trying to show confidence I didn't really feel, I waltzed into Station Twenty with a rosy, "I'm your new rookie!" pronouncement, to which I received four blank stares and a pregnant pause in reply. The silence was finally broken by a fire specialist with a rather frightening scar on his cheek and a voice that appeared to eke out of the scar rather than his mouth. "Well, did you bring the ice cream, Rookie?"

Proudly, like a child brandishing his first trophy in front of siblings who really don't care, I raised my bag of Blue Bell ice cream, shook it with a hearty hoorah, and said, "Two gallons of triple-chocolate!"

"Well, at least you got that right! Now shut up, stow your gear, and answer the phone if it rings." Welcome to Station Twenty.

I received my official station tour from another rookie who showed me where to stow my gear and helped me become familiar with the equipment placement on Engine Twenty. After a fair amount of time checking and testing equipment and studying the layout of the fire station, I was finally introduced to my company officer for the shift. To my twenty-two-year-old eyes he struck me as old, seasoned, and hard, with the wounded hands of a man who has seen too many long tours of duty, not to mention a litany of side jobs doing who knows what over the course of his career. I do know that he scared the wits out of me.

Just looking at him rendered me speechless, and I experienced two opposing thoughts as I stared at him wondering what to say: (1) *run away*, and (2) *I really, really want this guy to like me and respect me as a firefighter*. I decided on a safe remark: "Nice to meet you sir."

I'll never forget what he said in reply: "If we get a run, I want you to stick to me like white on rice. If I stop, I want you bumping into me. Don't make me look for you, okay?" His order struck me as a bit John Wayne-ish and frankly somewhat corny, but I said okay, he went back to his coffee and paper, and that was that. School over. Class dismissed. Go answer the phone.

The first half of the shift was pretty routine—study territory, clean the rig, police the grounds, drink coffee, lift some weights, and hope for the bell. Later in the evening, having just finished a round of full-contact ping-pong in the truck room with a bunch of firefighters whom I dared not beat (you better get off probation before you start winning in ping pong), I wrongfully thought that a shower was in order. This was my first introduction to firehouse practices in hygiene and was, in retrospect, a bad idea. During my shower, while humming a tune and minding my own business, I suddenly had a couple of unexpected visitors. Two firefighters fully bunkered out in their firefighting gear, tire brushes in hand loaded with Bippy soap (what we use to clean the rigs), generously decided to assist me in a personal scrubbing. I'm not quite sure how to describe the experience, but I do know for sure that I've never been so clean in my life.

That evening, long after dinner, with red cheeks and

a rather disturbing rash, it finally happened: We were just getting ready for bed and I was making the bunk next to the door (to quickly answer the phone if it rang), when the alarm bell jolted me upright. Actually, a more accurate statement would be to say that the alarm "tone" jolted me. In Austin, emergency crews are notified of a pending response with a rather annoying and anti-climactic tone, very similar to the sound that precedes the pronouncement: "Attention, Kmart shoppers." Having been raised on *Emergency* and *One Adam 12* and the tooth-rattling bell that always sent them on their way to great adventures and white-knuckled heroics, I was always somewhat disappointed by the dull tone of the Austin dispatch system. It just didn't seem right that the alarm wasn't, well, alarming.

I later learned that this tone was designed specifically to sound anti-climactic. Some study somewhere demonstrated that every time a tooth-rattling bell sounded in a firehouse, a firefighter's heart rate would double, triggering an autonomic nervous system response that shot epinephrine throughout his entire body. If the alarm proved to be false and the firefighter had no outlet for the adrenaline surge, over time, it was learned, this repetitive and instant rest-to-stress reaction led to a parade of ailments, including the number one killer of firefighters—heart failure. (Like old soldiers who jump every time it thunders, this is why most firefighters instinctively and uncontrollably flinch every time they hear a Kmart announcement.)

On this particular evening, though, I welcomed the sound because it represented the opportunity to face a new adventure, to apply my training, to brave the unknown, and to battle the extreme. I was ready and eager for adventure and had absolutely no idea what I was getting into.

The alarm came in on Manchaca Road, no less, just a couple of miles south of the station, and was dispatched as an "auto-ped." An auto-ped is simply jargon for an accident involving an automobile and a pedestrian, with the loser usually being the pedestrian.

Yes! I thought as I ran out to the rig and eagerly leapt into the jump seat, *this should be interesting!* Full of anticipation and nervous energy, I anxiously reviewed my medical training as we shot out of the station running Code Three, horn blaring to clear the traffic. Our flashing lights played an eerie dance on the oncoming vehicles and our sirens screamed our fleeting presence as we careened our way toward my first brutal face-to-face confrontation with the harsh realities of the career I chose.

Roughly ten minutes before the alarm sounded, just south of Station Twenty on Manchaca Road, this is what happened:

Jerry and Cindy were young and happy. They had spent a fun evening out on the town hanging out, partying, and enjoying each other and the company of friends. They both were buzzed from a few drinks and had plans to continue the party all night long. Traveling south on Manchaca Road in an old sedan, Jerry pulled out a nitrous oxide canister, a balloon, and a regulator for injecting the heady gas into the balloon—all the necessary ingredients of a "whip it" head rush (so named after whipped cream canisters that use nitrous oxide as a propellant). Cindy would fill the balloon and the two would take turns exchanging hits of nitrous oxide while Jerry drove. Like a couple of kids pulling on a helium balloon and giggling at the effect, Jerry and Cindy were screaming and laughing as they killed millions of brain cells in a powerful twenty-second rush that sent their young minds into a wild ride of hallucinations and psychedelic blasts of color and light.

After a particularly intense rush, Cindy passed the balloon to Jerry, rolled down the window, and stuck her head out into the moist June air. Jerry took a hit, laughed at Cindy as she leaned out of the car, and promptly lost control. Swerving right, Jerry's wheels rolled off the pavement, pulling the car off the road, forcing it into the grass and looming forest that lined the country road. In a panic, Cindy tried to pull herself back into the car, but the forces of the swerve actually forced her further out. Like a seatbelt that's been closed in the door, half in and half out, Cindy was stuck, head and shoulders outside the window, powerless to help herself. Jerry saw the trees coming and in a flash of clear thinking was able to yank the car left and back onto the road. Jerry took a deep breath as he realized that they had narrowly missed hitting a large tree, and was going to say, "That was close" when he looked right and realized that the same close call had removed Cindy's head in an explosion of pink mist.

We arrived on scene in two minutes. I jumped off the rig, grabbed the medical kit from the storage compartment, and, like a computer program stuck in a loop, kept repeating to myself, *white on rice…white on rice…white on rice…don't screw up, Rambo.* I was a little lightheaded and giddy from the rush of emergency response when I turned to find my lieutenant, whom I soon found standing at the passenger side of the sedan looking impassively inside, shaking his head and chatting with the paramedics, who beat us to the emergency scene.

My lieutenant certainly didn't appear to be in any hurry as he chatted to the paramedic by the car, but I scurried to his side anyway, eager to lend a hand where necessary. I glanced left and noticed the other paramedic checking on Jerry, who was morose and clearly in a state of self-induced terror.

I never even looked into the car. I didn't get a chance. As I neared my lieutenant, both he and the paramedic turned to me with a purpose and cut off my approach.

"It's a decap." My lieutenant said it in a dull, passionless tone, like an egg hitting the ground—no sound, just a thud.

"A what, LT?" I asked.

"A decapitation. As in no more head, Rookie. C'mon, we have work to do."

As we headed back down the road, my lieutenant asked me to get a couple of pairs of rubber gloves out of the medical kit. I grabbed two pair and handed him one, to which I received a crooked smile and a flat, "Both pairs are for you. Put them on."

We came upon the tree and he stopped, surveyed the ground, and commented that this must be the place. *What place?* I remember thinking. And then I saw it. Everywhere I looked there was a gooey mess, like a food fight in college where spaghetti is the order of the day—red, white, and pink mush was all over the tree, in the grass, and on the leaves—pieces of Cindy everywhere. You could easily see bone fragments, gray matter, and sticky ooze, the powerful lubrication of human bodies—deep red blood. The smell was strange. Sweet. Musty. Disturbing.

So, this is death, I thought. *Pretty ugly.*

In those days, the Austin fire academy was rather notorious for its extremely morbid, nonetheless strangely alluring, Faces of Death program. This full-day video and slide montage of Grim Reaper-gone-amok is a right of passage journey into death and its many faces (hence the name) and represents a shock-and-awe exploration into the depths of individual character. Here's the test: Just how much gore can you be exposed to without desperately crying out "Uncle!" The instructors watch you like hawks, not because they care about your inner child (who is freaking right out of his mind), but rather to see if you have the mettle for the job. "You will see this during your career, ladies and gentlemen. Get used to it."

As you watch the program, it's difficult to describe the experience: you want to shut your eyes and yet, strangely, you don't want to miss the next picture, and you certainly don't want your peers to see you flinch. The pictures are both disturbing and exciting, causing you to become riddled with guilt, not to mention nausea. The images of death cause a strange form of schizophrenia—you both do and don't want to see the next graphic picture of human tragedy. This mixture of emotions creates a bizarre stress cocktail that has one universal expression—hysterical laughter. "Did you see that, man? Oh, yeah, I need to see that like I need a hole in the head!" *Ha ha ha!*

Forced laughter is simply a vain attempt to hide the discomfort that comes with in-your-face reality. Ha ha. *Yeah, I can take it.*

But Cindy isn't laughing. I'm in the real world now. This is real death, and those are real body parts. There is a girl over there, what's left of her, who not ten minutes ago was breathing, laughing, and living. And here's what's left of her mind, pieces of Cindy's conscience spread out on the ground, sitting there in quiet repose, saying, *I dare you to touch me, Rambo.*

"We've got to pick all this up," my lieutenant said.

"Excuse me?"

"It's a crummy assignment, but we have no choice. Put on the gloves and get as much of it as you can into this bag. We'll wash down the rest. But get all the big pieces for sure."

I stood there in dumbfounded silence, truly not believing that he was serious, thinking this was a practical joke of the worse sort. *Pick up body parts?* I looked at the lieutenant with a quizzical frown, asking the question that I was afraid to ask out loud. He simply stared back, his message disturbingly clear: *I'm serious. Now get to work.*

Pick up body parts?

Like a Texas storm that appears out of nowhere on a beautiful summer day, I suddenly felt panic explode in my chest. Cold sweat. Rapid heart rate. Panting and wheezing. Hands shaking. As I reflect on the experience, I realize it wasn't really the parts themselves that scared me; it was the fear of how I would react to picking them up that scared the daylights out of me. *Will my lieutenant see my weakness? What if I get sick?* Such a close interaction with the pieces of death was just something I had not bargained for. *How will I react to this gruesome task?*

I tried my best to focus on the work and to control my breathing while I methodically put Cindy's brain in a Ziploc bag, but over time the smell and the reality of the event was just too much for me, and my fear became reality.

It began slowly. It started with excess salivation and then morphed into a clammy explosion of perspiration, and finally my stomach began to churn and rumble and send the alert that the contents were on their way out. I felt dizzy and drunk, in a fuzzy haze, outside looking in, like I was sitting on my shoulder watching the event take place and hearing my own futile screams, *No! This can't be happening!*

But it was, and there was no stopping it.

Not wanting to mix vomit with pieces of Cindy, and particularly not wanting anybody to see my weakness, I stumbled in a clammy stupor to the woods where, right on cue, I threw up twenty-two years of innocence in a series of gut-wrenching spasms that left me gasping between heaves, tears streaming down my face. Rambo indeed.

And that's when everything changed.

On my knees, in the woods, questioning everything I had come to believe about the career I had chosen and my ability to handle it, vomit on my chin and tears on my cheeks, I suddenly felt a hand on my back. The touch was reassuring—firm yet gentle, palm down between my shoulder blades, not pushing, not pulling—just a quiet reminder that "you're going to be okay." I looked over my shoulder to see my lieutenant, who looked like an old World War II sergeant with his helmet half-cocked and chinstrap hanging free. He smiled and said three little words: "You're not alone."

And I knew I had picked the right career.

THE POWER OF PURPOSE

It was my last shift as a "combat" firefighter. For almost fourteen years I had been making my living in the response arm of the fire service—working at fire stations, running on various rigs with varying missions, ascending through the ranks, transferring from station to station, and making emergency responses of almost every imaginable scenario. What's so exciting about combat life in the fire service is the very diversity of the events you may face from day to day. On any given tour of duty, you literally have *no idea* what you may be called upon to face. Imagine the infinite variations of timing, chance, and consequence—the stew of human error, stupidity, synchronicity, and intent—and you have the very complicated recipe for the firefighter's daily dose of potential challenges. I think it is for this reason that firefighters almost universally have come to refer to emergency response as "combat." Like combat, in the fire business you never know what you may get into, but you sure know it can kill you.

I'm not really certain when or where the association between firefighting and combat began, but the term "combat firefighter" is pervasive. It's also a badge of honor. Ask any firefighter you meet what he does for a living, and if he is assigned to a rig, he'll answer, "I'm a combat firefighter."[1] This association tends to knock the average person off balance, eliciting the obvious and ever-ubiquitous reply, "You're a *what*?"

"Com ... bat ... fire ... fighter."

"Why do you call it combat?"

Watch out. Now you've done it. You just invited a mission-obsessed individual to elaborate on the virtuous and noble calling of firefighting: to save lives and property.

Grab a cold drink and sit down because this may take awhile.

Far and away, it is the combat arm of the fire service that is most widely recognized (especially in a post-9/11 world). It's just hard to compete with the zeal and appeal of men and women riding on expensive red trucks, running into harm's way, and risking everything in order to help complete strangers out of trouble. Let's face it, fighting fires for a living is sexy.

But the truth is, like any modern organization, fire departments are very complex and diverse, with a multitude of non-combat jobs, responsibilities, and divisions. In fact, it is generally recognized that for a modern fire department to function efficiently today, you need roughly one non-combat position for every three on-duty combat firefighters. Firefighters have to be paid, trained, equipped, managed, housed, dispatched, clothed, and fed.

Buildings have to be designed and constructed safely, with modern fire and life safety features in place. Fire and building codes need to be crafted and adopted. High-risk occupancies and behaviors need to be addressed and corrected. Homeland security mandates need to be incorporated into policy and practice, and so on. Keeping a community safe in today's highly developed world is a serious and complicated business.

What *is* unique about the fire service, however, is that the majority of these non-combat positions are filled with firefighters. When a typical organization needs to create or fill an existing position, they generally look for an individual with special skills, knowledge, or training to fit the requirements of the job. Not so in the fire service. When you sign on to be a firefighter, you have to accept that over the course of your career, if you want to promote or advance, you are going to be asked to fill any of a number of non-combat positions. Many of these positions require special skills and talents that firefighters do not possess.

That doesn't matter, though, because if firefighters are good at anything, they are good at training; we simply train them to do the job. Like the designated "travelers" who are there to meet combat staffing requirements, all firefighters are viewed by the organization as potential "travelers" who can be called upon to fill necessary non-combat resource requirements. So, what you end up with over time is an organization whose leadership represents this gypsy-assignment construct of men and women who have moved in and out of combat and non-combat positions serving in various capacities and carrying with them the broader perspectives and skills they gained from the experience.

Regardless, even when you are a "combat" firefighter, the truth is, like soldiers, you rarely find yourself in a "real" combat situation. In fact, it's a fairly well-kept secret (one that most firefighters don't like to discuss) that fires in America are on a steady decline. Due to a host of improvements in building codes, public awareness, and firefighter training, the "big" structure fires—those that make headlines—just don't happen that often anymore.

So it was with a fair amount of complacency that I reported to work for my final shift as a combat firefighter. I simply didn't have very high expectations for the twenty-four-hour tour of duty. And even though I was well aware of the fire service folklore that the last shift is always the most dangerous—Murphy's Law is alive and well in the fire service—I didn't place much stock in it. The chances of having the Big One on this particular shift were just too remote. I was much more concerned with what to eat for dinner—or, more correctly, what to *cook* for dinner—as it is firehouse tradition to cook for the entire crew on your last shift before a promotion.

Timing and chance had a different plan, however.

At the time, I was captain and station officer for Fire Station Seventeen. I had recently competed for the position of battalion chief and had placed first on the promotional list, putting me in the hot seat for the next non-combat rotation. I knew that this shift represented a significant milestone in my career because once you reach the level of chief officer, you are pretty much out of the firefighting business. You may still receive a plum combat assignment, but at that level you're more manager and incident commander than firefighter. With this promotion, I had to accept that I wouldn't get my ears scalded anymore or experience the wild ride of dragon slaying. My days of "fire entry" were, by most standards, ending. It was not a big deal to me, though; I was weary of the response life, tired of getting up and down all night long and, frankly, ready for a new challenge.

Life as the captain and station officer at Firehouse Seventeen was always interesting. Every station and shift has its own unique personality—an oftentimes bizarre intersection of the various people who work there with all their attendant quirks and habits, tempered by the management style of its officers. Some firehouses can be quite tame and relaxed, with a studious bunch that prefer solitude and study as their twenty-four-hour fare. Other houses can be quite rambunctious, bordering on a twenty-four-hour fraternity party of horsing around and practical joking. Fire Station Seventeen was somewhere in the middle of these two extremes, and this particular shift was not much different from the countless shifts that came before it. Train, train, train. Eat, laugh, respond to medical calls, and *constantly* remind the men to behave.

John Green was the reason I had to monitor station behavior with an iron fist. John was the guy with the annoying giggle who would say in a whisper to a fellow firefighter, "Hey, what if we freeze his underwear and put them under his pillow. Wanna do it?" or "Do you think these slices of tomato would stick to the ceiling if we threw them just right? Here, watch." While I liked John as a person and even found some of his antics to be flat ingenious, John was a constant source of frustration to me because I was the station officer. It just seemed that John took great delight in testing the boundaries of authority, and I was deeply concerned that he would encourage the younger firefighters to take up his bad habits.

Because of this, I spent a lot of time knee to knee with Mr. Green counseling him to get his act together. Indeed, I would spend a significant amount of my twenty-four-hour tour at Station Seventeen reminding John that he was an adult and to please try to act accordingly. He would always look me in the eye, agree that he needed to improve, thank me for my wisdom, leave the room, and go tie the rookie up into a human pretzel. He was the master at rope craft. John really wanted to do good; he just couldn't resist the temptation to do bad. Just listen to that rookie scream.

John was a fire specialist, which is the driver rank in the City of Austin, and his assignment was to Ladder Seventeen as my driver. On the tailboard rode a young fellow and solid hand named Richard, a country boy who bred turkeys in his off time and kept the station loaded with freshly laid eggs—torpedoes for Mr. Green. The three of us constituted the entire crew for Ladder Seventeen, a unit whose primary mission was Search/Rescue and Forcible Entry.

Riding three firefighters on a combat rig is a very contentious issue. On the one side of the issue is economy and efficiency, the clarion call for government—doing more with less—and on the other is firefighter safety. Numerous studies have demonstrated that four is the optimal number of firefighters per rig, creating a redundancy that firefighters call "Two In, Two Out." The logic is simple: in a firefighting scenario, you should always work in teams of two, with a second team of two outside (or even inside) to assist you in the event you get into trouble. The hard lessons of experience have taught us again and again that when firefighters lose contact with their buddies or, even worse, work alone, firefighters die. This is why you will hear good fire officers always preaching to their crew to maintain "company integrity" while on an emergency scene. "Company integrity" is fire service jargon and its meaning is simple: stick together no matter what...*white on rice.*

However, fires don't happen that often anymore, and when they do, we send dozens of firefighters to the scene to control the blaze anyway. So, is it really necessary to pay for the increased staffing to meet four-person minimum standards given that firefighters aren't cheap? Indeed, for a major fire department, a standard of four-person minimum for every rig costs millions of dollars. You see the argument. To date, no side appears to be winning the debate, and both have valid points of view.

Regardless, with a three person crew, it's difficult to maintain the appropriate redundancy for firefighting operations. Somebody almost always ends up alone, usually the officer. And while John, Richard, and I had fought a number of fires together over the years, we had yet to really test the efficacy of a three-man crew—until this shift.

Firefighters learn to get a "feel" for a potential emergency response by the sound of the dispatcher's voice as he or she delivers the response protocol over the station PA. A dispatcher's level of concern tends to parrot the tenor and temper of the person making the call. If the tone is flat, sleepy, and boring, odds are pretty good that the person calling in the alarm isn't very panicked and the call will likely be false or not too terribly adventurous. However, if the dispatcher's voice is raised, alert and in a hurry, with clear descriptive elements such as "fire showing" or "child not breathing" then you know the odds are pretty darn good that you're in for a wild ride.

This box alarm[2] came in at almost exactly 3 a.m. In this case, the dispatcher's voice was up an octave and gravely serious as he gave the address to the Friendship Apartments on South Congress Avenue, a two-story housing complex that I was quite familiar with, having responded to a fatal fire there just a few years prior—a mother and two infants killed in a fire started by a cigarette.

The dispatcher made a final remark as we hastily jumped out of bed and into our bunker pants: "Multiple calls, heavy fire showing, possible trapped occupants."

Remember that the primary purpose of Ladder Seventeen was search and rescue. Such language will get your attention fast.

There is something strangely noble about fire crews getting ready for an imminent fight. You're all tensed up and moving with a well-orchestrated purpose: there's a steady, rhythmic movement of arms and legs as each firefighter jumps into his boots, pulls up his suspenders, buckles his trousers, and heads to the truck bay. It is extremely uncommon for anybody to say anything at this stage in the game. Each firefighter is lost in his own thoughts as he mentally prepares for the upcoming emergency. When I close my eyes and reflect on the experience of emergency response, what I remember are the sounds—the engines as the drivers start up the trucks; the comforting "click, click, click" of the overhead beacons as the flashing lights are turned on; the whisper of compressed air filling regulators accompanied by the harsh beep of the Vibralert as the firefighters don their breathing apparatus; the loud screech of the radio as the dispatcher repeats the call; and finally, when everyone is set in their seats, buckled in and tense, the sound of the overhead truck room doors rolling on their tracks as they slowly open up the gates to hell.

Since I knew that the Friendship Apartments were less than a mile from station Seventeen—an easy two minute response—I also knew that opening the bay doors would tell us definitively whether this was a real burner or not. As if in slow-motion, teasing us with their control over time and our destiny, the bay doors slowly revealed that we were in for a long night. When I saw the full view out the truck room doors, I swallowed hard, took a deep breath, and announced to John and Richard that they needed to psych up because the Friendships were on fire.

Firefighters call it the "glow." If you've ever had the opportunity to witness a structure fire at night, you know what I am talking about. At night, fire presents an eerie, reddish-orange glow that refracts off the very smoke it is generating. This refraction causes even small fires to loom large on the horizon, making firefighters swallow hard and sometimes miscalculate the magnitude of a pending nighttime structure fire. However, like beauty—a thing that is incredibly difficult to describe but we all know it when we see it—we all know the big ones when we see them. The night of the Friendship fire, the entire horizon was aglow, night turned to day by the careless act of one person walking away from food on the stove.

It took us 120 seconds to get there. Pumper Seventeen was first on scene, with Ladder Seventeen arriving right on its heels. Just behind me was a bull of a man and an incredibly talented firefighter named James Ash in Battalion Four, our chief officer and a very good friend. Chief Ash assumed command of the incident and immediately called for a third alarm, waking up the entire Austin Fire Department and moving dozens of men and women into action to lend a hand. While Pumper Seventeen began the arduous process of acquiring water for the fight, I surveyed the scene. What I saw both fascinated and frightened me.

Fire is a truly amazing natural phenomenon. Like a tamed animal, it can be our best friend or, when angered, our worst enemy, consuming everything in its path. The Friendship fire was a monstrous beast, burning with such incredible intensity that it was creating its own wind, sucking in air from the surrounding area to feed its insatiable appetite for combustion. If a fire has enough fuel and oxygen, it can burn with such ferocity that it creates a firestorm—a swirling tornado of fire and superheated gasses, spinning in a circular motion as it ravenously consumes fuel and oxygen. Like a freight train running off a bridge, a firestorm creates a cacophony that rattles even the most seasoned of firefighters.

The Friendship firestorm was horizontal, fifty feet in length and at least that in width; it reminded me of a colossal jet engine in afterburner. Blasting away at the arriving firefighters, the firestorm created a natural barrier of thousand-degree gases that blocked any easy access to the complex of residences. And just on the other side of this fiery plume were a bunch of sleeping people, unaware that their homes were suffering the most aggressive natural onslaught I had ever seen.

My first thought was RECEO, pronounced "ree-see-oh" by firefighters. RECEO is an acronym for fire scene priorities that every firefighter on the planet knows by rote: Rescue, Exposure, Confine, Extinguish, Overhaul. Never deviate from priority number one: rescue. People first, that's why we're here: to save lives and property. Ladder Seventeen's job: search and rescue.

"Search and rescue?!" screamed John in my ear. I shook myself from my scene assessment and looked at John, who along with Richard was fully decked out in protective gear, facemask in place, arms loaded with the accouterments of the trade: air pack, pick axe, hook, Halligan tool, belt axe, rescue rope, hand light, helmet light, carabineers, and assorted odds and ends. Both of them looked at me with determined expressions awaiting my orders.

I grabbed both John and Richard by their collars and pulled them close so that they could hear me and yelled that we were going to run around the firestorm and gain entry on the back wing of the complex behind the fire, from there get up to the second floor, and then start a methodical search of every apartment starting with the units closest to the fire. Both of them agreed with the order, fell into step behind me, and together began the jog around the raging firestorm. As we ran, I called to Chief Ash and told him our plan. He radioed back and wished us luck, assuring me that he would assign a hand line crew to support us with water as soon as possible.

The rear wing of the Friendship apartments was chaos. Police officers were kicking in doors to apartments on the far side of the wing, well away from the fire, yelling to sleepy residents to run for their lives. Pajama-clad residents were running in each direction, scurrying to get out of the way of the approaching fire. A police officer grabbed me and screamed that every apartment was occupied; there were people everywhere.

"What about those apartments?" he screamed as he pointed to the units closest to the fire.

"That's where we're headed," I replied. "Keep those people clear and don't get any closer."

The only stairway to the apartments closest to the fire was partially consumed by flames and was positioned just above and to the right of the main body of the fire. As we neared the stairway, John hesitated and looked back at me with a nervous "Here we go?" glance. I nodded to move as I snapped my regulator into place, and with Richard in his wake and me pulling up the rear, John charged up the stairs past the raging inferno.

The heat was tremendous. Even though we were each fully bunkered out in the best fire protective suits technology has to offer, you could still feel the intensity of the heat, which was sobering. In the old days, firefighters used their earlobes as Mine Canaries—the telltale sign that you were too close to the heat was when your ears started burning. So the saying went: "Ears burning? Back up!" Today, firefighters are so thoroughly encapsulated in protective equipment that they no longer have a "telling" first indicator that they are in too deep. Today, the only indication you are overheating is when you suddenly feel as if somebody just stabbed a beer tap into your chest and started draining your energy off in a torrential hurry. The fatigue that comes with overheating will drop a marathon-running firefighter to the ground in a matter of seconds. Going up those stairs I knew that our earlobes would be baking if they weren't so well protected.

I don't know about John or Richard, but on the way up those stairs, I was going through my "list." The "list" is something firefighters don't like to talk about, but is nevertheless a very real emotional response to extreme danger. Like a Matrix moment when time stands still and the dust hangs suspended in the air, the "list" represents a dilated moment in time when you recognize that the potential end is before you and you find yourself quickly running through a sequence of questions: Does my wife know I love her? Are our finances in order? When was the last time I thanked Mom and Dad for all the opportunities they gave me? Will the fire department be there for my family? I love the kids and will miss them…and so on. Hence the name: the "list."

The moment for the list passes as quickly as it comes, and once again you are before the dragon.

John and Richard didn't need to be told where to go; they were both seasoned firefighters and they knew the drill. On our hands and knees on the second floor balcony, we scurried under the fire, which was burning the eaves and roof above the closest apartments. We quickly made our way to unit 205, the apartment just adjacent to the firestorm, which was now raging through four different apartments. Without a second of hesitation, John smashed the front window of the apartment, allowing any heat and gases to escape, while Richard stood briefly and kicked in the door. As if it was in a race to see who could get to the occupant first, fire rolled into the apartment from the breezeway crawling along the ceiling, feeding on hot gasses and fuel, rapidly disappearing in the heavy black smoke ahead of us, which was roiling and boiling.

John screamed over his shoulder that he was starting a Right Hand search and was about to charge in the apartment when I grabbed his air pack. He looked back at me and I screamed, "I'm holding the doorway! Go fast! You don't have much time!" He nodded that he understood. Our three-man crew was finally put to the test. Richard grabbed John's air pack by the cylinder and, on their knees with John in the lead, they entered the apartment, right hands sliding on the wall for bearing, left outstretched to "feel" an occupant as they methodically searched the unit as a team. I remained at the doorway with one eye on the approaching inferno and the other on the smoky interior where my crew had just disappeared. Every fifteen seconds or so I would scream into the apartment while waving my hand light, "Here's the door! Follow my voice! I'm here!"

Watch the movie *Backdraft* and you get the impression that firefighters run into burning buildings with complete visibility, their chinstraps hanging free, coats unbuckled, baby under each arm, swaggering and heroic. That portrayal is not only wrong, it's terribly misleading, and even dangerous because it creates the misperception that you can see what you are doing in a fire. But you can't.

Look at your stovetop burner and you will see a form of efficient combustion, which simply means that you have an appropriate mixture of fuel with oxygen. But what happens when you have a problem with your stove and you end up with a "rich" mixture, or too much fuel (gas)? You get black sooty smoke. The smoke is essentially the unburned gaseous fuel—a product of incomplete combustion. A burning structure is a terribly inefficient form of combustion. Because a structure burns with such inefficiency, or incompleteness due to the amount of fuel, you get a tremendous amount of toxic black smoke when they burn. Even a small fire produces more smoke than can escape through the openings in an average structure. So where does the smoke go? Down. In a structure fire, visibility is almost always zero with floor-to-ceiling smoke.

If you want to know what firefighting is really like, try this: Go put on your heaviest winter jacket, pants, hood, and goggles; grab your scuba gear from the garage and put it on over your winter clothes; put a blindfold over your goggles; turn your stereo to its loudest setting, playing only static and noise; finally, turn your oven to 500 degrees and crawl in. Close the door.

That's what John and Richard were experiencing as they searched unit 205. The second you don't appreciate fire and its potential is the second it kills you.

While it seemed like an eternity, it only took John and Richard a few minutes to complete their search. With an incredible amount of relief, I saw John's helmet emerging from the smoke and in a second both firefighters were on their knees before me outside the now-burning apartment.

"Nobody in there, Captain," Richard said.

"Are you sure?" I asked.

"Pretty damn sure."

"Good work. Let's move on."

We quickly crawled to the next apartment, fire everywhere around us now. Once there I fumbled with my hand radio, cumbersome in my heavy glove. In the most urgent voice I could muster, I screamed through my facemask and told James that Ladder Seventeen was searching fully involved apartments and in desperate need for hand line support. He told me that they were working on it and to expect water soon. I looked around and couldn't see any helmets.

Now at apartment 206, we once again broke in the window and kicked in the door, fire racing ahead of us. I rapped John on the helmet and screamed, "We're almost out of time. I'm going in with you. I'll go right, you two go left. We'll meet somewhere in the middle." Two in, two out be damned. Both firefighters nodded and we were off.

Visibility in unit 206 was partial, with smoke quickly banking down the walls and fire running along the ceiling. On our knees we were under the heaviest layer of smoke and could quickly move through the rooms of the apartment. After completing my search of the living room and the kitchen, I bumped into John and Richard, all of us at the bedroom door entrance. We scooted in together. Richard went to the bathroom, John to the closet, and I went to the bed. That's where we found him.

Smoke has an intoxicating effect that actually causes a sleeping person to fall into a deep, and deadly, slumber. Our occupant was in such a stupor, and I shook him hard enough to rattle his teeth as I attempted to rouse him. John quickly joined me and together we pulled him out of bed and into our arms. I put my mask right to his ear and screamed that his apartment was on fire and we had to get out *now*. He looked at me in a terrified panic, but nodded that he understood. As Richard joined us, I took a good look at the front door. Fire was everywhere. The breezeway covering the balcony outside was on fire; the ceiling of the apartment was burning with tendrils down the walls like wicked fingers reaching for more victims—fuel. There was a window out of the bedroom, but we were on the second floor and the fire crews had yet to set ladders to the building. I had a hasty thought of lowering him on our rescue ropes, but quickly discarded the idea because it would take too long to tie him in a makeshift harness.

John screamed, "Let's shield him with our bodies and carry him through!" Not seeing a better alternative and knowing that nobody would survive if we didn't do something immediately, I nodded the okay. Together, the three of us created a human shield, enveloping our patient with our bodies and protective clothing, creating a human cocoon. I took a good look at each firefighter, a wordless command, and together we ran into the fire.

Our patient lived with only a few minor burns as mementoes of his experience. Funny, he didn't say a single word. Once we got him safely on the ground, like a spooked deer, he took off running, paramedics in close pursuit. My crew and I never saw him again.

After a quick group hug and a litany of "atta boys," John, Richard, and I went back to work and didn't stop until the six-alarm fire was under control several hours later.

The next morning I sat with my crew in rehab[3] drinking a gloriously hot cup of freshly brewed coffee. Laying down on our bunkers and smelling like a bunch of billy goats in a rut, John, Richard, and I kept reliving the experience. Like soldiers who just survived combat and are feeling giddy to be alive, we laughed like a group of kids as we compared our war stories from the morning's event. While sitting there, I saw James Ash looking around the rehab area, by now cluttered with dozens of weary firefighters. We connected eyes; he smiled and walked straight to me. As James neared, I noticed he had swelling tears in his eyes.

This six-foot, two-inch, 275-pound professional weightlifter and firefighter par excellence walked right up to us and without a word gave me, Richard, and John rib-splitting bear hugs. He stood back and looked at us and, in an emotional but deeply genuine voice, said, "Everybody is accounted for. No fatalities. You did it."

That's when I started thinking about sleep.

Remains of units 205 and 206 of the Friendship apartments in the background behind the firefighters. The crew of Ladder Seventeen rescued a sleeping occupant from unit 206 just as it began to burn. Five minutes later the occupant would have been lost in the resulting collapse. Picture by Bob Parker, taken from the Kevin Baum library.

LESSON FROM THE LINE
MISSION CLARITY

"You can be anything you want to be, do anything you set out to accomplish, if you hold to that desire with the singleness of purpose."

Abraham Lincoln

"Anyone can live heroically and successfully for one day. The man who achieves a high purpose makes that day the pattern for all the days of his life."

"Pep without purpose is piffle."

Authors unknown

I begin our leadership journey with the story about the fire at the Friendship Apartments because it illustrates what I believe to be the single most important element in the Firefighter Model that separates this industry from so many others—the Power of Purpose. Obviously, the

Friendship fire had a profound impact on me for many reasons and in many ways, and I have certainly given the events of that night some serious reflection over the years. However, over time, as I reflect on the Friendship fire and the incredible events of that night, one question keeps rising to the surface: What is it about the business of firefighting that causes men like John Green and Richard Kruse to put themselves in extreme danger and to demonstrate incredible heroics—indeed, put *everything* on the line—for a complete stranger? Why do they and so many firefighters like them engage in this pattern of behavior?

When you consider this question, it's easy to outthink yourself in the analysis, wondering whether it is the person who is attracted to the job that shapes the profession or if it is the profession itself, with its unique demands and challenges, that shapes the person. Like so many of life's complex questions, the real answer is, in my opinion, actually quite simple: *Firefighters know what they do and why they are supposed to do it.* Period.

Thomas Carlyle once said that a person who is gifted sees the essential point and leaves the rest as surplus. I believe firefighters have honed Carlyle's principle into a fine practice. While the firefighter's job can be incredibly complex (depending upon where he is assigned), the purpose behind that job is quite simple and universal: to save lives and property. That's it.

Save lives and property.

From day one in the fire academy and then throughout a firefighter's entire career, he is inculcated with this single purpose: *save lives and property*. Like a compass, he uses this purpose to navigate his career, carrying this mission with him wherever he goes. Indeed, ask a firefighter what he does and no matter where he is assigned, he'll respond by telling you the *purpose* of the organization: to *save lives and property*. Even if he is a building inspector, the firefighter knows that the purpose behind those inspections is to *save lives and property*. Budget officers provide materials and products so that we can *save lives and property*. Training officers provide skills, knowledge, and abilities to firefighters so that we can *save lives and property*. Even someone like John Green, who is seemingly incapable of focusing in the firehouse, once on an emergency scene demonstrates an impressive ability to channel his actions into productive labor to *save lives and property*. (In fact, the guy is a bona fide hero—one of the most decorated firefighters in the department).

Because of this focus, a firefighter doesn't lose sight of his true purpose very easily; or, as Carlyle notes, a firefighter gets the essential point behind his professional existence and then lives it.

This lesson is extremely important and one that organizational leaders today should seriously consider. Here's why: It is the *operative* purpose behind an employee's actions that drives employee and group behavior. Leaders, either tacitly or overtly, establish that operative purpose with what they say, do, value, and reward. What is the *operative* purpose in your organization today? What is the *operative* purpose in your life today?

Here's an exercise: Go ask an employee of your organization what he does, and, very likely, that's *exactly* what he will tell you—what he does. "I'm a claims manager."

Go ask a firefighter what he does and he will not only tell you what he does, he'll also tell you *why* he does it—"to save lives and property."

The distinction between these two answers is critical to this leadership discussion. A typical employee when confronted with this question discusses *practice* ("I process claims"); a firefighter discusses *purpose* ("I save lives and property").

It appears as if so many of today's organizations have lost their compass, the alignment between the *why* and the *do* in the organization's stated purpose. This misalignment between the *why* and the *do* is, in my opinion, a failure point in organizational leadership, one that can become quite problematic over time. In fact, I think we see examples of this misalignment every day in the way we are treated by employees, in the design of processes and systems to support customer transactions, in the way we automate for efficiencies, and in the way we recognize and reward our employees.

Here's an example: What is the purpose behind Dell computers? Is the purpose to sell millions of computers, or is it to make millions of computer users happy and satisfied every single day? If the perceived purpose is to sell millions of computers and increase quarterly earnings, then we are likely encouraging deviant behavior in order to meet this goal. "It doesn't matter whether the computer user is satisfied or not; in the end, we just want to sell as many computers as we can!" This operative purpose (real or imagined) is what will drive employee behavior.

Here's another example: What is the purpose of your

insurance company? Is the operative purpose to make money, or is it to protect you from damage and harm? It is the operative purpose that will *drive* employee behavior, and that purpose will be revealed to your customers by what you do, say, and don't do. In time, it is the *operative* purpose that will define you and your organization, not the glitzy words you have on plaques hanging on walls.

If you want your employees to show great fortitude and courage in delivering your mission, you probably need to make sure that they know what it is and then execute that mission through leadership action. Remember, it is the *operative* purpose behind an employee's actions that drives the behavior. So *be careful* what purpose you are communicating and putting into practice in your organization.

Some elements to the Firefighter Model that you should consider as you reflect on your organization's operative purpose include:

- Clarity of purpose: There is minimal ambiguity in the purpose that drives the Firefighter's professional behavior—to save lives and property. This purpose is easily understood, is never altered by new management regimes, and is simple. I am absolutely convinced that it is the very *simplicity* of this stated purpose that makes it so easy for a firefighter to focus, and thus put it into operation. Indeed, to the extent that we complicate an employee's life with multiple and often competing professional mandates do we make it increasingly difficult for them to focus. This lack of focus results in inconsistent employee behavior, which frustrates customers, confuses the workforce, and decreases productivity. If you want your employees to focus, make the object of that focus something they can understand.

- Unity of purpose: Saving lives and property is the stated and operative purpose for the *entire* organization, regardless of a firefighter's particular assignment or function. This stated purpose—to save lives and property—is the "red thread" that ties together the multiple and varied functions that make a modern fire department work so well. This unity of purpose creates a powerful synergy that drives collective behavior toward a common goal and reduces the destructive competition that can stem from siloed thinking (where one part of the organization competes with another).

- Shared Purpose: Like the Marine Corp motto—"Once a Marine, Always a Marine" firefighters are trained to be firefighters first and then they take that perspective with them throughout their entire career, no matter where they are assigned. Embedded within that very perspective is the power of purpose—we're *all* saving lives and property, even if we aren't assigned to a combat rig.[4]

DARE TO CARE

Fire Station Six, located on South Congress Avenue just two miles south and across the river from the Texas State Capitol, is a very old and rustic house located in what was once the seedy part of town. As a rookie, I can remember sitting on the front bumper of Ladder Six, dangling my feet in the air, wagging them to and fro and smiling—wide eyed—as I watched the prostitutes work the street right in front of our station. I don't know if the station made them feel safe or if the firehouse brought them good luck, but they seemed to spend a great deal of time in our front lawn. It was fun to exchange jokes with them, jibes back and forth about the size of our fire hoses, fire trucks, and ladders. Even though they always seemed friendly and happy enough, I couldn't help but feel sorry for them, wondering what twisted path led them to their chosen profession.

Providing the perfect backdrop to this unfortunate inner-city scene was an old theater-turned-triple-X with ridiculous movie titles emblazoned on the brilliantly lit marquee, proudly announcing the even more ridiculous plots you could enjoy if you dared to enter. In a seemingly defiant act against authority, the prostitutes would work their trade in the very shade of the Capitol's great shadow, right in front of a fire station lit up by the triple-X marquee. Take that, Authority.

Today South Congress Avenue is a perfect example of good policing and urban renewal. If you want to see an example of inner-city revitalization that works, go visit South Congress Avenue in Austin (now rechristened as "SoCo" by the chic clientele the area attracts).

Long before all this renewal took place, however, I cut my teeth as a budding firefighter on the streets and neighborhoods that surround Fire Station Six and South Congress Avenue and learned a good many lessons about the career I chose and the people who live it. Among the many lessons I learned during this three-year assignment as a rookie, perhaps the most valuable was this: *If you will just stop, observe, and listen, you can learn a great deal from your peers and colleagues.* I was first introduced to this important lesson during my early experiences in hydrant maintenance, and I even remember the exact fire hydrant—that wicked little plug located at the corner of South Congress Avenue and Academy Road.

Fire hydrants are a fundamental element in every city's infrastructure. Even though the average person probably does not, from day to day, find himself giving fire hydrants much thought, they are nevertheless quite important to their safety; without fire hydrants, an *entire* community could very easily burn right to the ground. Indeed, in the "old" days, the central most vexing problem firefighters faced during a structure fire was how to get water to the fire. Ever heard of a bucket brigade? Bucket brigades were lines of firefighters and volunteers who, during a fire, would shuttle buckets of water from person to person—like an inch worm slowly moving the hump to the tip—until the water reached the unlucky chap at the end, who threw it on the fire and frequently burned himself in the process (probably a rookie).

There are three fundamental ways you can extinguish a fire: (1) remove the fuel, (2) remove the oxygen and smother the fire, and (3) cool the fire. Water is hands-down the most effective tool we have to fight structure fires because it both cools *and* smothers most fires.[5] The water itself cools the fire while the expansion of water to steam smothers the fire (at 212 degrees, water expands 1,700 times its original volume when converted to steam—an incredibly efficient conversion ratio for smothering a fire). This is why a skillful firefighter can extinguish a heavily involved attic or basement fire with one short blast from his one-and-a-half-inch fire hose—the rapid expansion of water to steam fills the entire space and smothers the fire in a matter of seconds. Water damage is limited and the fire is out. Pretty cool.

The fire service lives by water and has come a long way since the days of the bucket brigades. That fire plug you see out front represents the visible portion of what is a fascinating and oftentimes confusing underground network of pipes, valves, and pumps, all designed to shuttle water from sources of supply to sources of need. And since water is very important to a firefighter, so is that plug you see out front. That plug represents the firefighter's cherished source of water, and the supply hose we carry on our rigs serves as our modern-day bucket brigade.

For this reason, most fire departments have a regular program of hydrant maintenance, where the firefighters police the hydrants in their response territory to ensure proper functioning; nothing is worse than arriving at a fire scene and finding that the hydrant does not work. As a rookie, it was my job to do the majority of this maintenance work, or so I was told.

Eager to please, one summer day in 1985 I found myself at the corner of South Congress Avenue and Academy Road staring at the place where our plug was supposed to be. Somewhere under a dense canopy of brush, bushes, and weeds was our fire hydrant. My lieutenant harrumphed and told me that this particular hydrant was considered a bother by the home owner and that they consistently planted brush to "hide" the unsightly device. Apparently they had limited appreciation for the plug and its value to them as homeowners.

"Doesn't matter what they do," remarked my lieutenant. "The hydrant belongs to the city. Let's clean up the brush and test the plug, but hang on a second there, Rambo."

I only heard the first part and, like the Tasmanian Devil, leapt into the brush, shears flashing and limbs flying as I cleared the weedy rubbish from around the hydrant. Occasionally I would hear one of my crewmates chuckle and try to interrupt my melee, "Uh, Rambo, you may want to slow down a bit there." But being the good soldier I was, I would ignore them, desperate to gain their appreciation as a hardworking brother. Finally, they were all laughing at me, pointing fingers, and commenting,

"Way to go there, Rambo!" "Now you're doing it brother!" Occasionally they would throw me the necessary tools to complete the job—wrench, grease, washer, sealant—always shaking their heads and smiling at the silly little rookie covered in the weedy refuse of his organic combat. I probably even looked like Rambo, all covered in greenish camouflage, streaks of dirt on my face, clothes, and limbs, dust floating in the air stirred up from my aggression. I thought their laughter was good-natured camaraderie and appreciation for my hard work ethic and can-do spirit.

I was having the time of my life. I love this job, man! Look how much fun we are having!

The truth is my buddies were laughing at me because the homeowner had apparently planted poison ivy around the hydrant in order to "prevent" someone from clearing the brush—someone like me, I suppose—and they had been trying all along to warn me, I just wouldn't listen. In my haste to impress, I had jumped right into a world of hurt.

Even though the story of "Rambo's Losing Fight with the Poison Ivy" eventually made it to the Fire Station Six Darwin Hall of Fame, the next seventy-two hours were hellish for me. Literally covered head to toe in poison ivy rashes, I spent the remainder of that shift and the next few days under the watchful care of my station buddies. While they thought the event was knee-slapping hilarious (I would have too, given a role reversal), they had no idea my physical reaction to the ivy would be so dramatic. Within twenty-four hours my welts were oozing puss and I couldn't move my limbs without terrible pain. At night I would wake having ripped the gooey scabs off in my unconscious haste to scratch the itchy mass. All the while,

Lessons from the Line

my crewmates were calling and coming by, asking what I needed and how they could help, apologizing for not warning me, having their wives offer remedies, and generally extending to me a level of care that a fellow can only find from his spouse or his mother.

The depth and level of their concern for a stupid young rookie who ignored their pleas and got himself into trouble was touching and it made a powerful impact on me. When I finally returned to work after my ugly battle with poison ivy, I began to watch my station buddies with a new interest, wondering about the level of genuine care they gave me and asking the obvious question: do they just like me or do they demonstrate this level of care to anybody who is in need? Do they *really* care or are they just being nice?

In fact, I spent my entire career observing my peers with this question in mind.

It is interesting what they taught me when I started to watch and listen. What follows are two short stories. Read them and answer the question for yourself. Do firefighters really care, or are they just being nice?

Mrs. Jones was a sweet elderly lady who lived alone in the neighborhood surrounding Fire Station Six. I don't know Mrs. Jones' story, how she came to Austin, if she had family or was ever married, and so forth. But I do know that from time to time, Mrs. Jones needed help and there was nobody in her life to help her—that is, except for the firefighters of Fire Station Six.

I think our first experience with Mrs. Jones was when she

had a water leak in her house. In a panic, not knowing what to do or whom to call, she dialed 911 and asked for help. Even though the fire department is not in the plumbing business and technically the department has no obligation to respond to a water leak, water *is* something firefighters know well, and the dispatchers could tell that Mrs. Jones was frightened. So they dispatched Engine Six on a Code One (no lights or sirens) "service" call to check on Mrs. Jones.

When we arrived at Mrs. Jones' home, a 1930s bungalow not far from the firehouse, we quickly discovered that she had a broken toilet. While the officer talked Mrs. Jones through her crisis, the rest of us mopped up the mess and fixed the leak. Mrs. Jones was beside herself with gratitude. "I didn't know who to call. I was so frightened. You boys are wonderful!" She offered cookies and other goodies and promised to visit the station for a tour.

Mrs. Jones never came by the station that I can remember, but every other month or so she would have an "emergency" and we would be dispatched to her home on a service call. We would get to her home and she would tell us that there really wasn't a big emergency, "And in fact I'm feeling quite better now. But since you boys are here anyway, would you mind too terribly getting my Christmas boxes out of the attic?" We would happily oblige and offered to move the furniture around so that she could set up her tree. We would always ask Mrs. Jones what else there was to do around the house, and she would readily produce a short list prepared for the occasion. The firefighters considered it a labor of love—after all, she could be anybody's grandmother, even our own.

Over the years, as I traveled around from station to station throughout the city, I realized that every fire station has one or two Mrs. Jones' in their response territory—that person or small group of people that the firefighters have adopted. When you look at these relationships, what is common among them is that the firefighters are essentially giving "free" care to somebody in need—somebody who needs someone, who has nobody to turn to. The firefighters aren't doing it because they have to. They don't. They are doing it because they *want* to; because they genuinely *care* about the person and their plight and take the necessary time out of their day to lend a hand.

I specifically remember a fellow in Fire Station Fifteen's territory, an east Austin firehouse. This poor gentleman suffered a severe weight problem and couldn't lift himself out of his bed for even routine activities such as using the restroom, cooking, or changing his clothes. Not knowing what to do, he started calling the fire department for service assistance. The firefighters would respond and, in a caring and deeply respectful fashion, help this challenged fellow to accomplish his goals. Over time, the demand for this service reached a level that began to concern the firefighters. Rather than tell this poor gentleman that he needed to find alternate care for his needs, the firefighters worked with the County Medical Director to *find* the service for him. I never heard the final disposition of the man's case, but I do know that the firefighters were not willing to let him face his challenges alone.

I could share countless little vignettes of firefighters helping strangers when they didn't have to—a choice to lend a hand because somebody needs one. Whether on duty or off, firefighters almost universally share a deep and genuine desire to help their fellow man in times of need. Why do you suppose that is?

Today pre-hospital medical care is the primary response demand of a fire department. Generally speaking, seven of every ten emergency responses today are for pre-hospital medical care. Of the remaining three, fire is only a fraction of the demand—the others being any of a number of emergency events from hazardous materials spills to wilderness rescues. Even though the repertoire of a firefighter's daily grind is limitless, if you look at the data one trend stands out in stark relief: the bread and butter of a fire department today is medical emergencies.

Because of this trend, fire departments today are increasingly well equipped and staffed to meet the demands of pre-hospital care. In most fire departments, every firefighter is trained as a basic emergency medical technician, which means they have the training to render life-saving aid to patients in the field, such as CPR and external defibrillation, bandaging and splinting, patient assessment, and so forth. Additionally, select firefighters are trained as advanced emergency medical technicians (frequently referred to as paramedics), which means they not only can render aid, but also can deliver essential life-saving medications to patients in the field, a key element in the pre-hospital care system. Together, the two levels of training serve as an extremely effective tool for pre-hospital emergency care redundancy. No matter what your illness or injury, a fire department today can elevate its level of response with the appropriate complement of trained firefighters to meet the demands of the emergency.

Station Six's response demands mirrored the national trend and, generally speaking, whenever the alarm sounded we assumed we were on our way to another medical call. Most medical calls in Six's territory were "routine," meaning they represented emergencies that firefighters see a lot, such as drug overdose, difficulty breathing, minor injuries, and traffic accidents. It was rare, say one in fifteen, that we went on a medical call that was out of the ordinary or that truly challenged our skills. But it did occasionally happen.

I don't remember the exact date that the little boy fell off the eighth-floor balcony in the downtown hotel, but I do know it was in the summer. We were out back playing basketball, which at Station Six was more like football with a round ball. Even though I tried to approach the sport with a good attitude—especially since my officer was addicted to basketball as *the* best sport for fitness training—the truth is I hated it. I hated it because I don't like the sport much and I probably don't like the sport much because I'm terrible at it. I can remember playing until dark, wishing the whole time that the sun would go down so that we could stop, only to have my officer say, "Hey, ya'll wanna keep going? We can set up the truck lights and play all night."

Ugh.

So it was with a tremendous amount of relief that I heard the tone go off that day out back at Fire Station Six. *Finally, a break from this stupid game,* I thought.

The alarm came in as a "Fall." Fall calls are very common in the fire services; in fact, falls are the number-one cause of injury in the home. (Think about that the next time you climb your ladder to hang your Christmas lights!) All sweaty and smelly, we jogged to Engine Six, jumped into our bunker pants, climbed the rig, and were on our way. The downtown hotel was just a mile down the road at the river, and our fall victim was apparently in the hotel. Bread and butter.

But this wasn't your typical fall. The downtown hotel, like so many modern hotels, was designed with a magnificent multi-floor atrium—a cavernous open space where the room balconies and walkways face in, rather than out. Apparently, while attending a wedding reception, a young fellow, around seven or eight years old, had accidentally become separated from his mother and father. Nobody really knows how he got to the eighth floor; speculation is that he tried to get up high to find his parents, and while leaning out over the balcony to see better, lost his balance and fell, cart wheeling down to the lobby floor.

While we were en route, I practiced my medical call ritual: based on the defined call, a fall, I expected to see a broken bone, maybe a laceration, a headache, and an embarrassed patient. I reviewed my training for this type of a call, yawning as we headed down the road. Halfway there, my lieutenant opened the sliding window that connects the front cab of the rig to the jump seat where I was riding. "Hey Kev," he said. (Rambo silliness—and *all* silliness, for that matter, goes away when the bell tolls.) "Dispatch just told us that this is a fall from the eighth floor—a kid. Sounds serious." I sat straight up.

We were at the hotel in no time, only to find the parking lot jammed. Our specialist, an aggressive driver nicknamed Waffalow[6] barked a complaint that he couldn't get to the front door. My lieutenant yelled over his shoulder, "Get the medical kit and get inside any way you can. We'll be there as soon as possible."

I jumped off the rig, grabbed the medical kit, and ran to a side entrance to the hotel. Through the door and into the maze. I saw a sign for the lobby and jogged down the hall. As soon as I entered the lobby, somebody saw me and yelled for me to follow. Together we ran to the center of the atrium, where there was a small crowd of spectators forming a circle around the little fellow. I muscled through them and found him crumpled on the floor, arms and legs akimbo, Mom crying at his side and Dad on his knees in a terrible state of frustration because he didn't know what to do. The boy looked like my nephew, which knocked me off balance for a split second while I quickly did a mental inventory of my own family members.

I quickly recovered and realized immediately that the boy wasn't breathing. You could hear the gurgling sound as he suffocated on his own blood. "We're here. Scoot over and let me help," I said as I put my hand on Dad's back, having learned from my own experience how comforting it is to have somebody touch you when you are in a panic.

Dad looked at me with tear-filled eyes and sputtered, "Will he be okay?"

I looked Dad in the eyes, scooted in beside him, and said, "I'll do everything I can to help him."

I ran through the patient assessment priorities. AB-Two-C,

I thought. *Airway. Breathing. Circulation. Cervical Spine. Airway: check the airway first, if obstructed, clear it, open it, allow air through the windpipe. Breathing: once the airway is cleared, is there breathing? If not, begin to breathe for the patient. Circulation: once you are moving air, is the heart beating? If not, begin CPR, because no amount of air in the body will help if the heart is not moving it around. Cervical spine: if you have an open airway, breathing, and circulation, in trauma always immobilize the spine and prevent further injury.*

These priorities, like RECEO, are sequential and go in order of importance. Never deviate.

The boy wasn't breathing and it was obvious his airway was obstructed. His chin was on his chest, spinal fluid coming out of his ears, blood oozing out of his mouth. He couldn't breathe. Gently, I used a trained method to slowly reposition the boy's head to open the airway while not causing further damage to his cervical spine. Still not breathing. *Dammit, where are the other guys?* No time to fuss over proper airway treatment, this boy needs air *fast*. In violation of medical scene protocol, I began to give the little fellow mouth-to-mouth resuscitation. Lips to lips. Body fluid to body fluid.

Back in the early 1980s the emergency services were really just beginning to learn about blood borne and airborne pathogens—those scary little germs that can jump from host to paramedic through the air or through contact. We had received a couple of classes about a disease that nobody could pronounce but was shortened into an acronym called AIDS. It sounded serious. Because of it and many other disease processes that were emerging as threats to first responders, the department had issued a host of medical scene protocols, chief among them to protect yourself first. Surprisingly, protecting yourself from air or contact-borne diseases is pretty easy—wear gloves, glasses, mask if necessary, and use extreme caution with any and all body fluids.

But at the time of this call, we were just learning to protect ourselves and, frankly, I didn't think there was any time to spare. I began breathing for the boy—my lips to his, my air to him, my oxygen to his vessels. As I breathed for him, I checked for a pulse and found one. The heart was still beating very faintly, but still there, now hopefully with life-saving oxygen in the blood.

Waffalow and my lieutenant finally arrived. My lieutenant looked at me with a stern but understanding glance as he saw what I was doing while he and Waffalow promptly prepared the oxygen and airway device for mechanical, external breathing. We set it up and started pumping 100% oxygen, trying to get life-saving air to the little fellow's vital systems. We immobilized the spine and kept working. Even though the young fellow had obvious fractures of his limbs and God knows what internal injuries, for a patient in this kind of condition—imminent danger to life—you have to focus on the primary ABCs and then start thinking about transport to the hospital.

It's called "triage," and it is *much* more difficult to execute than you may think. Remember the movie *Saving Private Ryan*? Right after the initial beachhead, the doctor is moving from wounded soldier to wounded soldier and telling an orderly where to place each patient in the order of triage. Even though he would occasionally come across a conscious patient, he would nevertheless triage that soldier as "dead" because of the severity of his injuries. In triage, you not only have to assess the *extent* of the patient's injuries, but also you have to assess the likelihood that intervention will *save* them. If you use what limited resources you have on hand to help a patient who has suffered mortal injuries, you may cause another patient's recoverable injuries to become mortal due to a lack of timely attention. Triage is how you prioritize multiple patients, and it is a wickedly complicated business.

But triage is not just an activity to prioritize multiple patients. You also have to employ the exact same principle to individual patients who have suffered multiple injuries. It's tempting to walk up to a patient with an obvious fracture of the femur—the bone in your thigh and a serious break—and immediately begin work on traction, bandaging, and splinting. However, if the patient also has also suffered an injury to the chest and is filling up with blood, he is going to rapidly deteriorate regardless of your efforts with his femur because you have prioritized the order of the severity of his injuries incorrectly.

This little fellow had so many injuries that it was difficult to determine what to address next. The best plan was to package the entire body on a spine board and get him on the way to the hospital as quickly as possible, which is exactly what we did. Nonetheless, it is hard to do so when you have obvious injuries that are begging you to splint them, and it hurts your entire psyche to have to move a broken bone without splinting it first.

Perhaps not surprisingly, when loved ones begin to witness the urgency of a medical scene event, they begin to lose control. You would think that the presence of trained professionals would soothe them, but for a loved one who is a bystander, the feeling of helplessness can become overwhelming, and it usually comes out in fits of emotion. Understandably, Mom began feeling this helplessness just as the paramedics arrived with the stretcher. While one of the paramedics began an IV, the rest of us packed the boy for the quick ride to the hospital. Speed is extremely important in pre-hospital care, and we wasted no time getting the boy on his way to the emergency room.

On our way out of the hotel, I saw one of the paramedics put his arm around Mom and whisper into her ear. Together they walked behind the stretcher. The paramedic consoled the parent as she searched in his eyes for any signal of hope, comfort, confidence, or encouragement. The paramedic looked back into her eyes—*your emergency is our emergency*—and with genuine concern and empathy, said, "Your son's condition is serious but he is in good hands. We know what we are doing. We're here for you and we are going to do everything we can to help your son. The doctors at the hospital are the best in the business and they are waiting for our arrival."

"Thank you," said Mom.

I've seen it over and over again over the course of my career: a firefighter or a paramedic will touch an aggrieved loved one or share soothing words with a patient, and they instantly calm down, sometimes smile, and always say thank you. They are just words and simple gestures of care—holding a hand, a touch to a back, an arm around a shoulder—but they are given out of a heartfelt empathy for the victim and the family, an expression that we are all in this together. I'm convinced that it is not the words or the contact that make the difference so much as it is the acknowledgment that you are not alone; that there are people sharing this experience with you doing everything possible to ensure a good outcome. *You're not alone.*

Later at the fire station the mood was subdued. Nobody wanted to play ball anymore and we all sat in front of the television in the day room with thousand-yard stares, not really watching the program, each lost in his own personal struggle to put the event into perspective. For me, I couldn't get the taste of his blood and the texture of his lips out of my mind. I brushed my teeth a dozen times; yet every time I closed my eyes I could hear the gurgling, taste the bitter copper of his blood, and feel the smoothness of his lips. It haunted me. It still does to this day.

For the rest of the guys it was a mixture of emotions—some thinking of their own children and wives, others brooding on the senselessness of the accident. I was left wondering what else I could have done in those first three minutes, haunted by the possibility that I didn't do the right thing to save the little boy. Would he survive and, if not, was it my fault?

The rest of the fellows at the station, those who didn't make the run with us, would sit with us and ask us to talk about the call. They were attentive, caring, and empathetic. All silliness was gone. They would touch us slightly to let us know that, "Yes, sometimes this job can suck, but we're all in this together and you are not alone."

Events like the boy on the balcony remind the firefighter how fragile and fleeting life is; how quickly a great day can turn into a tragedy; how bad things can happen to good folks in the blink of an eye. And because of this, the firefighter goes home and tells his wife he loves her, sits and watches the kids as they sleep, plays fetch with the dog, calls Mom and Dad, and is both patient and caring with rookies who jump into beds of poison ivy. But most importantly, the firefighter recognizes that tragedy could just as easily happen to him and he learns to treat each and every "customer" as he would a member of his own family. He does this because the firefighter is smart enough to know that tomorrow their emergency could just as easily be his.

LESSON FROM THE LINE
SERVICE COMMITMENT

"I don't know what your destiny will be, but one thing I know: the ones among you who will be really happy are those who have sought and found how to serve."

Albert Schweitzer

"People don't care how much you know until they know how much you care."

Author Unknown

"Too often we underestimate the power of a touch, a smile, a kind word, a listening ear, a compliment, or the smallest act of caring, all of which have the potential to turn a life around."

Leo F. Buscaglia

A couple of months ago I was in Washington, DC, trying desperately to get to Orange County, California. True to form, I had booked my week with minimal room for error; I had to get from coast to coast in one night and be on the ground working with a client in California first thing the following morning. My itinerary was to take a quick commuter flight from DC to Chicago, and there pick up a jet for the four-hour ride to Orange County. The flight from Chicago was the last of the day. I had to make it.

If you travel a lot, you realize very quickly that fate can play some funny tricks on you. I've learned that the best days for travel are when you are *not* in a hurry—everything always seems to go smoothly. It's when you are in a hurry—when you *have* to get from where you are to where you want to be—that everything seems to fall apart. I *had* to get to Orange County, so not surprisingly, my commuter flight was two hours late.

I sat and sat and sat and became increasingly frustrated and concerned as I waited for my commuter flight to arrive. Most of my travel companions were in a similar predicament, and we were all whining about where we had to be, how much time we had on layover, whether we would make it, and what was going on with our flight. Finally the plane arrived. We boarded and sat and sat and sat. I got the flight attendant's attention and asked why we weren't moving. I was informed that the baggage handlers were still loading the plane. "I fly all the time and it never takes this long," I whined. Sorry, sir. I politely asked him if he wouldn't mind telling the baggage handlers that everybody on the plane was in a hurry and to please step up the pace. He looked at me like I had Vienna sausages sticking out of my ears and walked off.

We finally took off and made our agonizingly slow commute to Chicago. Like a bunch of robots stuck in a power surge, all the passengers were looking from their watch to the window to each other, grimacing—big sigh—back to their watch, window, each other—big sigh—and repeat. Just before our arrival to Chicago, our flight attendant told us that an airline representative would be awaiting us at the gate to lend a hand with connections and sorry for the hassle.

We finally arrived, and quickly formed a line in the jet way to wait for our carry-on bags, which you couldn't carry on when flying this particular commuter. We waited and waited and waited. Finally, I asked the jet way representative if she wouldn't mind yelling outside to the baggage handlers to tell them to hurry up because our flight was two hours late and we were all in a big hurry. "They are moving as quickly as they can, sir." I looked outside and the handlers were laughing and watching as one person slowly removed the bags from the plane.

I looked at my watch…the window…big sigh. Repeat.

Of course I was the last one to get his bag. *This is becoming funny now*, I thought as I zoomed up the jet way to meet the airline representative, who was not there. In fact, nobody was there. The gate was deserted! In a flash, my grin quickly turned into a frown as my emotions morphed from frustration to anger. I looked around for some help but there wasn't any. Like the guy who wakes up and finds he is the only person left alive on the planet, I had a vision of myself screaming "*Hello?*" only to have it ricochet around the concourse and fall flat in front of me.

Not knowing what exactly to do, I ran to the terminals, hoping beyond hope that my connection was also late. It was gone. On-time departure. *Uh oh.* I started scanning the board looking for a flight, *any* flight, to Southern California. There was one left to Los Angeles. *That will work,* I thought. *I can rent a car and make my hotel by midnight.*

No time to spare, I looked around and saw a gate attendant working a nearby gate. I sprinted up to her; my briefcase, like a dog being yanked around on a leash, was threatening to break as it struggled to keep the pace. In front of the attendant, panting, I quickly told my story and finished with an urgent plea: "Can you help me get to California?"

The attendant lifted a crooked finger and pointed over my right shoulder to a wall, three gates down, where a bunch of people were congregating. "Sir, you need to go over there and use the red phone to address your needs."

I slowly looked to where she was pointing and with great care looked back at her, smiled, and said, "Madam, there is a long line over there and as you can see I'm in a very big hurry. I have to catch that flight to LA. I'm here, you're there, nobody is behind me waiting, and I need some help. Can't *you* help me?"

Deadpan. "Sir, you need to use the red phones." Crooked finger.

"I don't want to use the red phones. I want to use a human. And frankly, madam, I wouldn't be here if your airline had not been late. I realize that you are not the cause of the delay, but you can certainly be a part of a solution. Won't you help me?"

Blank stare. "Sir, you need to use the red phones."

My final remark to her: "Madam, one day you will find yourself on this side of the desk in my position. When you do, how would you like to be treated?"

Her final remark to me: "Haven't you heard, sir? Customer service is dead in this airline."

How do you respond to that? As I contemplated her final remark, staring in disbelief, I turned toward the now infamous red phones, wondering whether I could use them to call my client with the bad news.

I share this story as an introduction to this lesson—and as a comparison to the fire service stories that came before it—because I believe strongly that experiences like the one I had with this airline are becoming increasingly common in today's fast-paced world. Whether we are traveling, purchasing, ordering, calling, driving, or simply asking for assistance, it appears as if the recipients of our requests are becoming increasingly impassive at best; at worst, downright uncaring and rude. Why do you suppose that is?

Here is a fun exercise: Ask your friends and colleagues if they have ever had a similar experience to my airline story with any business. Then ask if those experiences are an increasing element in their consumer experience. I think you can guess the answer.

Now compare this trend to the behavior you experience when you call the fire department. Have you *ever* seen a

Lessons from the Line · 81

firefighter that didn't appear to genuinely care about you, your condition, your emergency, your life?

Let's turn the conversation around. Have you ever had an employee of a Fortune 100 company come by your house and unpack your Christmas decorations, simply because he knows you can't do it for yourself? Do you suppose your employees stay up at night wondering how they could have provided better service to a customer in their time of need—indeed, haunted by the experience and their role in it? What *is it* that separates the fire service profession from so many others when it comes to customer service, genuine concern, and empathy? How can the stories I shared with you at the beginning of this chapter—and I could write an entire book of such stories—be so radically different from our daily consumer experience?

While there are a number of possible explanations for this disparity, I believe the answer lies in a simple principle that can be extracted from the Firefighter Model—a principle that shapes this profession and the behavior of its professionals. Here it is:

> Firefighters do not simply provide a service. They are *a participant in* every consumer transaction and, because of this interaction, develop a deep connection with and empathy for their customers.

Spend much time in the fire service and you quickly realize that life has a way of balancing the playing field when it comes to emergencies. It doesn't matter who you are, how much money you make, whether you are educated or not, important or not, male or female, young or old, black or white, nerdy or sophisticated. If Murphy decides to pay you a visit, you are going to become a victim in search of assistance. "Emergency" is an equal-opportunity predator.

Over the course of a career, then, a firefighter will experience emergencies on numerous scales—human, environmental, structural, and financial. And, while a firefighter over time may become somewhat casual toward the whimsical nature of Mr. Murphy, he never loses touch with the human element in this transaction because *he is always intimately involved in his customer's emergency.*

Think about that for a minute.

It has been stated that the average person will require the services of a fire department approximately once in a lifetime. If you've already had the pleasure of this experience, you know that it was a powerful influence in your life. You talk about it, relive it, tell stories about it, learn from it, brood about it, and reflect on it during sleepless nights. (If you have not had the pleasure of this experience, don't worry, you will.)

However, a firefighter has a similar experience multiple times per shift, hundreds of times per year; and in every single case, he is living your once-in-a-lifetime experience with you!

Firefighters are *not* just simple observers to your emergency—spectators to the consumer transaction. Firefighters are active participants, living the experience with you, feeling the emotions, sweating, bleeding, and crying; they are vital partners in your unfolding drama. Indeed, in many cases, your emergency literally becomes theirs, such as when a firefighter becomes lost while searching for a trapped occupant in a house fire. Because of this deep interaction with and role in the multiple facets of human tragedy, a firefighter learns very early in his career a single powerful lesson that influences not only his worldview, but also his entire approach to his career and the quality of service he delivers: *It can happen to me.*

It can happen to my wife, my mother, my sister, my brother, my best friend, me.

It can happen to you.

A firefighter, because he has been an active player in so much human drama over the course of his career, walks in a constant state of anxious awareness—that strange and esoteric knowledge that comes from the repeated and constant backhanded slaps of reality: tragedy can happen anytime, to anybody, even to me. If you don't believe me, go observe a firefighter as he listens to the radio as an emergency unfolds on a street near his home. He is tense, alert, fearful, wondering again and again, *Where is my wife supposed to be right now? The kids? Why won't she pick up her cell phone?* He doesn't fully relax until he has accounted for his family and close friends. This tension is not because a firefighter is fatalistic; he is not. It is because he has been taught by the brutal hand of reality, over and over again, that accidents do happen—to anybody.

A firefighter, because of the nature of his work, understands a very simple but profoundly powerful principle of customer service: treat your customer as you would like to be treated if this was your emergency, or consumer transaction, because tomorrow it very likely could be.

This is precisely why a firefighter stops by to lend a hand to a stranded motorist, helps his neighbors without being asked, volunteers to visit elementary school children and discuss fire safety, unpacks Christmas boxes for lonely old ladies, holds the hand of a patient while his comrades splint a broken bone, and treats you with complete compassion and sensitivity when you have your emergency.

Ms. Jones could be my mom (or yours); how would you like her to be treated? The boy that fell from the balcony could be my nephew (or yours); how would you like him and his family treated? The panicked man who missed his flight could be my brother (or yours, Red Phone Lady!); how would you like him to be treated? The next rookie to ignore his peers and cover himself in poison ivy may be your son; how would you like him to be treated? The next person to pick up the phone and dial 911 could be *you*; how would *you* like to be treated?

If you want your employees to care about your customers, to show genuine compassion and empathy for their needs and concerns, indeed, to receive hugs from total strangers, as a leader you should constantly remind them of two basic truths in the Firefighter Model, truths that all firefighters know by rote:

1. You are a *participant* in the consumer transaction, not an observer; and

2. Tomorrow *you* may be the person on the other end of the line dialing 911 (or across the counter).

How would *you* like to be treated? Think about it.

GIVE UP THE NOZZLE

Friday the thirteenth of December 1996 is a day I will never forget. On that fateful day, the City of Austin experienced one of its worst structure fires in recorded history, burning an entire city block of three-story condominiums to the smoldering ground. The Centennial fire (so christened for the name of the complex) was a $13 million structure fire—a total loss—that made more than two hundred University of Texas students homeless in a night, destroyed dozens of vehicles, caused more than four additional structure ignitions due to burning brands, and took hundreds of firefighters to control. That fire took days to put out. I know because I was there. In fact, I was in charge, an unlikely position, given that I was only a captain and chiefs are supposed to be in charge of fires.

The day of the Centennial fire I was assigned to Battalion One. For firefighting purposes, the City of Austin is gerrymandered into five geographic regions called "battalions," and each area is under the supervision of one battalion chief.[7] That chief officer is the regional boss for the battalion and his or her word is the spoken gospel from on high, the voice from the clouds that calls you at shift change and tells you whether your day is going to be sunny or a rainy hell. The battalion chief supervises all the fire stations and firefighters in a battalion and decides who does what for the shift—who rides what rig; who travels where and who stays put; training assignments; and duty assignments.

The battalion chief is arguably the critical cotter pin that links the combat arm of the organization to the policy arm of the fire department, the guy or gal who orchestrates all the necessary activities that make a modern fire department work like a well-oiled machine. And like a cotter pin, take out the battalion chief and the machine will quickly fall apart.

Here's why: Firefighters don't just sit around waiting for emergencies as so many people erroneously believe. Over the course of a typical shift, a fire crew will respond to calls, report for training, inspect buildings, conduct pre-fire plans of high-risk buildings, attend training schools, drive territory, train rookies, test equipment, travel back and forth to fill in staffing gaps, and complete any of a host of other routine tasks and errands. Fire crews are constantly coming and going over the course of a shift and, as they do so, the company officer will call the battalion chief and report their movement. It is the chief officer who has to ensure that at any given point in time, his battalion is *response ready*. Think about that. If nobody is minding the house and all ten crews within a battalion are engaged in some non-emergency activity, what happens when somebody dials 911 in the geographic region? What if there is a real emergency?

Most people do not consider the tremendous amount of logistical effort that occurs behind the scenes to keep their fire department running. They drive by a fire station and see the rig in the garage and breathe a sigh of relief—that comforting feeling anchored in the knowledge that there is a safety net out there hanging in place, there if they need it, ever on the ready. But the truth is that safety net is constantly being re-spun over the course of a shift. Like a group of conductors trying to orchestrate a symphony that is fragmented between multiple music halls, a modern fire department represents a strange webbed network of chief officers bartering and horse trading between battalions to fill in staffing gaps, response holes, and readiness demands, all so that when you have that once-in-a-lifetime emergency and dial those three magic numbers, the right number of trained firefighters, on the right rig, will be at your home in eight minutes or less. So next time you drive by that fire station and see the crew in quarters, give a silent salute to the coordinated efforts that make it possible.

As you can imagine, providing the right standard of coverage[8] for a major city can be a terribly complicated business, and the day of the Centennial fire was no exception; in fact, staffing and coverage was an absolute nightmare.

I reported for duty at ten o'clock that morning and took one look at the staffing board and knew I was in trouble. Since Friday the thirteenth was just two weeks before Christmas, I knew that many of my senior officers would be off on vacation and I expected the typical spike in sick-leave use, but what I saw on the staffing board was a frightening spectacle of "Who's on first?" gone nuts. In a gesture of good will, Chief Cooper, the A-shift battalion chief, had tried to manipulate my board as the sick leave calls had come in that morning, but had finally given up in frustration. He laughed at me as I stared at the board, slapped me on the back, and guffawed as he headed to the locker room. "Welcome to my world, KBaum." He smiled over his shoulder, "Merry Christmas!"

Thanks.

In Austin, chief officers organize their battalion personnel with a staffing board of sliding name plates. Each firefighter's name is differentiated by color (rank) and assignment (station). Since chiefs are constantly moving personnel around the battalion and the city over the course of a shift, the board gives the chief a quick, at-a-glance visual of current staffing levels. As I contemplated Chief Cooper's holiday cheer and stared at my board, what initially caught my eye was the absence of color. Captains are in charge of ladder companies and their names are in red; lieutenants are in charge of engine companies (pumpers) and their names are in orange; and drivers and firefighters are represented simply by the color yellow.[9] What I saw that morning as I stared at my board was a sea of yellow. The majority of colored name plates were temporarily slotted into the "Vacation/Sick Leave" panel, meaning that most of my officers—and most of the battalion's experience—were off duty.

In most organizations, when a supervisor takes a day or two off—or a week—their work simply piles up and is left unattended until they return. To my knowledge, it is rare that employers require someone else in the organization to tackle an absent supervisor's workload while they are gone. Rather, we simply receive the auto-e-mail reply telling us that so-and-so is out of the office and when we should expect his or her return. Occasionally we are given a name of somebody to call in their absence, only to have that person tell us to please wait until so-and-so returns because that is really so-and-so's area, not his or hers.

But you can't do that in the fire service. The fire business is a twenty-four-hour, seven-day-a-week commitment whose mainstay consumer demand is emergencies. When it comes to emergency service, somebody always has to be in charge, every rig has to be staffed, every station has to be open, and people have to be trained and ready to respond. Emergencies don't care if it's a holiday or your turn to be on vacation, nor, frankly, do you if it's your turn to have an emergency. In the fire business, somebody *always* has to take the place of an absent supervisor or firefighter. Always.

Study the ancient practices of Roman soldiers and you can find the origins of the fire service's response to this staffing challenge. Roman soldiers would fight in a phalanx—a disciplined group of soldiers organized in the shape of a large square. Each "square" was comprised of lines of soldiers, one behind the other, usually several soldiers deep. This phalanx would meet an enemy army head on in a clash of swords and shields, and the soldiers up front would "hold the line" as they took the fight to the enemy. As soldiers on the front line would fall, the soldier in the line just behind would move up to fill in the gap, never allowing a weak spot or a hole to break the strength of the line. As front-line Roman soldiers became fatigued, they would be replaced by the soldier just behind them, allowing them to move to the rear of the phalanx to rest, eat, drink, and get ready to re-engage in the fight. By the time they reached the front of the line again, they were fresh and ready to take the fight to the enemy.[10] Like a human accordion, Roman soldiers would process through the phalanx, slowly moving from the rear to the front and back again. This practice took fierce discipline but, when executed correctly, proved to be an incredibly effective method for destroying an enemy.

In the fire service we hold the line through a practice called "Higher Classification." Here's how it works: When a firefighter of a higher rank (driver, company officer, chief officer, etc.) is off duty, a firefighter in the rank immediately below the absent firefighter will plug the hole by stepping up into his or her position for the duration of the absence—a shift, a week, a month—whatever the timeframe may be. That firefighter is then working in a higher classification than his assigned rank, hence the system's name.

Here's the best part about higher classification: for the duration of the firefighter's tenure in higher class, he is paid the wages of the absent officer and receives all the perks and privileges attendant to that rank. Pretty cool. But there's also a challenge: for the duration of the fighter's tenure in higher class, he is also expected to know the demands and expectations of that rank and to do everything that the missing officer would and should do were he present. Everything.

While this may sound like an easy transition, in practice it is much more difficult than it sounds. Think about it. For every rank in the fire service, a firefighter has to be cross-trained to meet not only the challenges of his current rank and assignment, but also trained to meet the demands of the rank and assignment immediately "ahead" of him. In other words, every firefighter has to be cross-trained in the duties and responsibilities of both his job *as well as* that of his supervisor. Indeed, the day a firefighter is promoted to lieutenant, he celebrates the event by cooking his peers a steak meal and then heads back to the study room and starts sharpening his knowledge on the rank of captain because next shift he may be asked to become a higher class officer for a day.

Akin to our Roman ancestors, firefighters today are constantly moving back and forth in the staffing "phalanx," swapping positions and responsibilities and jumping in and out of higher classification(s) in order to hold the response line. This is why you will never hear a 911 dispatcher tell you, "I'm sorry, but that station is closed today because the officer is on vacation. Will you please call back next week?"

I was working in higher classification on Friday the thirteenth of December 1996, a captain temporarily assigned to the position of battalion chief. While I had served as a chief officer a number of times, I had yet to cut my teeth on a large fire or incident; and, frankly, I had mixed feelings on whether I really wanted to. I had studied all the books, knew all the protocols, and understood the responsibilities of the rank. Yet I was still somewhat hesitant to "wish" for the Big One. I was keenly aware that being the incident commander (IC) of a major fire is radically different from being a company officer. As IC, you're not just in charge of a crew, you're in charge of several crews. Depending on how large an incident gets, that number can become very large, very quickly. The IC makes the decisions about strategy, tactics, scene assignments, and acceptable risks. Indeed, his decisions determine the ultimate outcome of the incident as it is his strategy that is being applied. In emergencies, the buck—and the burden—rest with the IC.

While the demands of being a chief officer are certainly heady and I never took them lightly, I still took comfort in the knowledge that there is great redundancy built into a large fire department. We design them that way. In a large fire department, there are usually more experienced officers somewhere within shouting distance that you can lean on if the going gets real tough, and the larger an incident becomes, the more likely it is that you will see some of these officers come to your aid. I always knew that if I got into a real jam, I could reach across the city to find some assistance.

Studying the board that day I realized that this shift was going to be somewhat different, however. By the time

I had manipulated the board, horse-traded with other chiefs, and authorized mandatory overtime, it became apparent to me that just about every station in my battalion—and, in fact, the entire city—was going to be commanded by firefighters working in higher classification. Perhaps even more alarming, as I studied my board I slowly realized that I was one of the most experienced and senior officers working that shift. *No time like the present,* I thought. *I can handle it. And besides, what are the odds that we'll have the Big One today anyway?*

Before I closed the final details on the day's lineup and headed downstairs to eat lunch, I made a quick call to my buddy James Ash in Battalion Four deep in south Austin as a security blanket and to bolster my nervous bravado.

"How does it look down there, James?" I asked.

"Pretty grim. Lots of vacation and sick. Paying a hell of a lot of overtime. How about you?"

"Same." I paused, then asked hopefully, "Hey, you're going to be here all shift aren't you, James?"

"Yeah, why?"

"Just making sure. I may give you a ring if I need some help."

"Feeling a little jittery there, Kev? No problem. Call me if you need me. You know you're not alone."

Twelve hours later, just before midnight on Friday the thirteenth, I was calling James Ash like my life depended upon it, because as far as I was concerned, it did.

It's hard to say exactly when the Centennial Condominiums began to burn. Here's what we do know: At around 2 p.m.

on the afternoon of Friday the thirteenth, Pumper Three, which is stationed just a half-mile down the road from the condominiums, was dispatched to the complex on a trash fire. The "acting" lieutenant on Pumper Three was a strapping fellow named Mike O'Donnel—one of those guys you expect to see on a firefighter's calendar and the type that all women swoon over. Tall, handsome, and smart, Mike had recently been promoted to driver, but today found himself working as a lieutenant. Friday the thirteenth was his first shift in higher class as an officer—his maiden voyage.

What Mike found when he arrived on the scene was a dumpster fire in the basement parking lot, built directly underneath the condominiums. Not a big deal, as dumpster fires are very common. Mike and his crew easily extinguished the rubbish fire and began the process of mopping up. As Mike was inspecting the area around the rubbish fire, he noticed that there was a trash chute directly above the dumpster. The chute was a convenience for the tenants, who could throw their rubbish down the chute from any floor to the dumpster in the basement. Mike correctly realized that the chute acted as a chimney that could easily transport heat and gasses up into the structure, so Mike and his crew moved the dumpster in order to see inside the chute. When Mike looked up, he saw fire.

I was finishing up some paperwork at headquarters when the box alarm came in for the Centennial Condos. Headquarters is not too far from the campus area; running Code Three (lights and sirens) on side streets, I made my way to the complex in less than five minutes. Mike met me on the street.

"Chief, we had a dumpster fire that extended to a trash chute just above it. I think we have it out but the chute runs all the way to the attic. We need to get our guys on each floor and into the attic to check for fire extension."

"I agree. Head on up and I'll send Ladder Three to meet you on the upper floors with the thermal camera."

While technology has made a number of advances in the way we fight fires today, perhaps the most impressive improvement to the firefighter's repertoire of tools has been the Thermal Imaging Camera (TIC). Through the use of infrared technology, the TIC enables a firefighter to "see" heat differentials between and within objects—warm objects appear as bright spots in the viewer, and cooler objects are dark. For example, at room temperature, a person will appear as a bright white human outline and a fire will appear as a brilliant white object. Conversely, when a firefighter is searching for a lost victim in a structure that is burning, if the room temperature is over 100 degrees, which is very common, a victim's outline will now be dark compared to the white background. The device shows heat differences, so it's important that the person using the camera knows what he is doing.

Weighing several pounds and designed like a massive pair of binoculars, the TIC has revolutionized how firefighters check for spot fires. Fire loves to hide in walls, ceilings, and difficult-to-reach places. In the "old days," a firefighter would make an educated guess on where a fire might be hiding, based on what he knew about the principles of heat transfer and then start tearing down walls to see if he was right. Frequently he was wrong, which meant he had to tear down more walls to try to find his hiding fire.[11] As you can imagine, this was an incredibly inefficient and destructive, albeit necessary, process.

The TIC changed all that. Today we simply carry thermal cameras around and "look into the walls." Any sizable hot spot hiding in a wall or ceiling will give a heat signature, marking the exact spot where the firefighter needs to explore. Tear out the wall, put out the fire, minimize the damage, and finish the job.

While the crews were canvassing the upper floors and attic of the Centennials with their TICs, I set up my command post on Twenty-sixth Street, just outside and in front of the complex. A command post, while absolutely necessary, can be a lonely and boring place when the fire is out and the excitement is over. Standing on the street with my headset on, chatting with my firefighters by radio as they continued their search, I had plenty of time to examine the Centennial Condominiums.

Built in the west campus area and part of the University of Texas city-within-a-city Empire, the Centennial Condos were a magnificent three-story congregate resident facility designed specifically for students. Covering an entire city block and configured in the shape of a massive H, with a courtyard on each side of the bridge, the facility reminded me more of a five-star hotel than a complex for student housing. As I looked at the building, I couldn't help but to shake my head and laugh. My old dormitory days were the slums compared to where these kids were living. What particularly caught my eye was the private entrance. Similar to a gated community, the Centennials had one entrance to the entire complex—a gate off Twenty-sixth Street. Each corner of the complex housed stairs to reach the upper floors, but to get to them you had to enter through the main gate off of Twenty-sixth Street. The single entrance struck me as odd, and I remember thinking it would serve as a significant challenge in a real fire.

Two hours later, after an exhausting and thorough search of every floor and nook and cranny where fire could be hiding, I officially closed the incident at the Centennial Condominiums and released all the units from the scene. We never found a hot spot or any indication that the rubbish fire had extended into the structure beyond the chute.

As Ladder Three drove by on its way back to the fire station, a buddy of mine yelled out the window through a toothy grin, "See you tonight at the Big One, Chief!"

"No you won't!" I harped back. "I plan on sleeping tonight!"

Just before midnight on Friday the thirteenth, I was roused from my sleep with the following alarm:

"Box Alarm, 501 West Twenty-sixth Street, Centennial

Condominiums, reported heavy fire, all units respond on FireCom 1. Multiple calls."

As we hit the pole hole to slide down to our rigs, the acting lieutenant of Engine Two looked back at me with a concerned expression and quipped, "Did we miss one?"

I just shook my head.

As I approached the Centennial Condos that night, I began my "Hot Lap" from the windshield of the car. Incident Commanders are trained to make a quick visual of a burning structure from as many sides as possible before establishing a command post. Called the Hot Lap, this quick visual is extremely important—especially when dealing with large buildings—because the situation you find on one side of a building can be radically different from the situation you find on another side. In order to establish a sound fire suppression strategy, it is important to know what is going on from as many vantages as you can. Usually, the Hot Lap can be completed on foot. However, since the Centennials spanned an entire city block, I decided to drive mine. If I was having any trouble shaking the sleep out of my system up to that point, my 360-degree survey of the building served as an ice-cold wake-up splash to the face.

Here is what I saw on my ride: A heavy glow emanating from the center of the structure, indicating that somewhere in the middle of the complex the fire was venting freely, exposed to open air and oxygen; soffit lines under the eaves of the roof that had burned out, exposing a red glow lurking in the background, indicating that the attic was on fire; vehicles parked on the street and everywhere around the structure, inhibiting fire apparatus placement and indicating that the complex was heavily occupied; students looking out their windows trying to figure out what all the commotion was, oblivious to the fact that their building was on fire; and finally, as I established my command post in the exact same place as earlier that day, I noticed that *nobody* was exiting the building from the front, indicating that the students had not been notified and that we were up against the most profound search and rescue challenge of my career.

Before I even stepped out of my car, I issued the following order over the radio:

> Battalion One is out on the scene, I'm assuming command and my command post is on Twenty-sixth Street at the entrance to the building. I have a three-story, multi-family residential complex, wood frame construction, fully occupied with fire venting out the roof and heavy fire involvement in the attic. Search, rescue, and evacuation are a priority. Dispatch, sound a third alarm, with special request for Battalion Four response.

With this one order I woke up the entire Austin Fire Department, the city manager, and the mayor; initiated hundreds of pager alerts; scrambled more than twelve additional pieces of firefighting apparatus with their crews (including James Ash), all running code three to the incident; and caused the fire chief and his command staff, who were celebrating together at a Christmas party, to put down their cocktails, look at their pagers, and ask the obvious, "What's going on downtown?" Thirty minutes later they would be able to tune in to CNN to find out.

Even though it probably does not look like it to a casual observer, a fire department's response to a structure fire is actually quite organized. Depending on the sequence of a unit's arrival on the scene, each responding piece of apparatus and crew has a pre-assigned role. Generally the first arriving pumper and ladder go directly to the scene to establish command and give incoming units a verbal description of the incident and their planned initial actions such as fire entry, rescue, or initial suppression. Frequently it is the initial actions of these first-in crews that set the stage for the remainder of the incident.[12]

The second and third arriving pumpers go directly to fire hydrants and await the order to "lay in" a supply line of hose. The second ladder establishes a staging area and awaits additional orders from the IC. This second ladder company will usually be assigned the task of RIC Team—Rapid Intervention Crew—meaning that they stand by, fully decked out and ready to enter at a second's notice to rescue a downed firefighter. The RIC Team's sole purpose is firefighter rescue. Finally, the special rescue company reports directly to the IC to assist with command of the incident. Nobody needs to tell a crew what to do as they approach the scene; they all know the drill.

In the case of the Centennial fire, I arrived at the same time as my first-in crews. As I stepped out of my car, like before, Mike, officer of my first-in pumper, was there waiting on me, eyes wide but determined.

"Mike. You got the water on this one. Pull your bundle, get it inside, and see if you can cut this fire off. I'll have Pumper Two lay to you. Everybody else is going to be working on search and rescue. This whole place is occupied. Protect the guys as they work. I don't know how long it will be before I can get more lines in there to help. Get on it!"

"Yes, sir!" Mike yelled as he scurried off to get his crew and pull the lines.

As I was setting up my command post at the back of the vehicle, I radioed Pumper Two and told him to lay a five-inch supply to Mike's rig. I also called Pumper Nine, my third-in hose crew who was not yet on the scene and instructed him to get to the scene as soon as possible to assist with the rescue efforts. I then made the radio call to Ladder Three and told the officer to position his rig at the southeast corner of the structure for possible master stream application, but as soon as possible to get inside and evacuate, evacuate, evacuate! Ladder One was my second-in search and rescue crew, and I wasted no time telling them to get to the scene and get inside. All this took about five minutes.

It is commonly accepted in the fire service that the first five minutes of a fire are the most important. It is in the first five minutes that you establish your strategy—offensive, meaning an aggressive interior attack of the fire, or defensive, meaning you are going to fight the fire from the exterior. It is in the first five minutes when you identify if you have trapped occupants and initiate rescue efforts. It is in the first five minutes that you apply your first streams of water. How and where you apply these first bursts of water can have profound consequences on the outcome of the incident. It is also in the first five minutes that you position your apparatus around the structure for future use.[13] Finally, it is in the first five minutes that a fire can grow from a manageable burn to an out-of-control conflagration.

In the first five minutes of the Centennial fire, I had set the stage for the remainder of the event. My strategy: rescue, rescue, rescue. I used almost all of my first-in resources in the search and evacuation of the students from the building. In doing so, I knew that I was essentially allowing the fire to grow unchecked until I could muster the resources to mount a serious suppression effort. Poor Mike and his crew were my only attack lines, and I was crossing my fingers that he could get inside and nail the seat of the fire quickly, or at least hold it back while the other firefighters completed their rescue work.

Unfortunately, the Centennial fire had a different plan.

While I was out on the street giving my initial orders and moving people into position, the fire inside the Centennials was ravenously consuming everything in its path. It had already found a common attic to play in, and like a kid in a candy store had run around unchecked gleefully tasting everything in sight. Having started on one of the lower floors in the bridge of the H, by the time we reached the scene the fire was already burning on three floors and had penetrated both the elevator shaft and the storage rooms that were located on each floor of the bridge. Unknown to the firefighters, the second floor storage room was where the condominium staff stored several gallons of paint thinner—an extremely flammable liquid. As Mike and his crew were stretching their attack lines into the Centennial courtyard, attempting to get just past the fire in order to cut it off, one of the cans of paint thinner in the storage room failed from heat exposure. As this first can failed, it sent a mist of super-flammable gases into the maw of the fire causing a rapid and explosive chain reaction that ruptured all the stored cans of thinner. This reaction blasted massive holes in the elevator shaft, sent burning brands soaring in each direction, rocketed a fiery plume of super-heated gases and fire into the attic, and catapulted the elevator car out of its housing as it went crashing to the bottom.

Mike had just pulled his lines past the elevator lobby, which was located in an outside breezeway on each floor of the H's bridge, when he was knocked on his back by the explosion, fire and heat washing over him like a rolling wave. Reeling from the impact, Mike looked back at the breezeway and realized in dismay that the explosion had caused a partial collapse of the bridge and the debris had landed right on top of his hoses, cutting them off completely and rendering them useless. Mike pulled on one section of hose, hoping to yank it free, only to have the whole section come away, severed by the collapse. Like a skillful enemy carefully setting the trap and pulling it at the perfect time, the Centennial fire had masterfully thwarted our only initial effort to get water on the fire and, in the process, had accelerated its expansion rate by an order of magnitude.

On the street the explosion sounded like a dull rumble—a small earthquake or thunder rolling in the distance. I looked up, saw the fiery plume, and immediately called dispatch to initiate a fourth alarm. *More resources, more resources, more resources*, I was thinking. I was about to initiate a roll call when I saw Mike come stumbling out of the front entrance. He came straight up to me, strong but shaken, and told me the bad news.

"Can't we get *any* water on the fire, Mike?"

"Not from this entrance, Chief. It's completely cut off by the fire. I lost everything in there—all my equipment and my hoses. Gone. Frankly, I'm lucky to be standing here."

I took a good look a Mike and smiled—another courageous firefighter. "You okay, buddy? All your body parts still attached and your crew accounted for?"

Mike gave me a weak smile, "Yeah, I'm fine. A bit shaken. My crew is right over there. What do you want me to do now?"

"Report to Ladder Three and give a hand with rescue. Be careful!" I shook my head in admiration as Mike stumbled off. *He'll make a fine lieutenant one day*, I thought.

As I stood at my command post and watched Mike head back into the fray, I had a fleeting thought that I was in way over my head. *This scene is rapidly unraveling*, I thought. *How many people will die before this night is over?* The radio broke my musings, and I quickly admonished myself for the self-doubts and began to re-think my suppression strategy. No time for silly notions; there will be plenty of time for that later.

I stood on the street looking up at the Centennial complex wondering how in the hell I was going to get water on this fire. The fire was now burning fiercely, sending a twisting plume seventy-five feet into the air. I could see firefighters in the stairwells shuttling nervous students past the fire and out of the building. I specifically remember watching as the crew from Ladder One kicked in doors on the third floor, pulled shaken kids out of their apartments, and then ran them under the fire to the stairs. *Way to go guys!* I thought. *You can do it!*

I radioed Ladder Three to get an update on the rescue efforts. His report was sobering, but encouraging, "Every apartment is occupied. We almost have the third floor clear and are working down."

"Is it possible to get cut off lines in place?"

"Not from where we are, IC."

"Okay. Let me know as soon as you clear the third floor. I'm going to start elevated master streams to hold the fire."

"Roger that."

An elevated master stream is a powerful tool in the firefighters' arsenal of suppression strategies. Modern ladder companies are equipped with a hydraulic ladder that can be raised a hundred or more feet over a fire. Engineered into this massive ladder is a standpipe, which telescopes in and out as the ladder is raised or lowered. Supplied by a pumper, ladder crews can attach a five-inch line to the rear intake, which feeds into the standpipe, enabling them to blast more than a thousand gallons a minute on a fire from the nozzle at the tip. All master stream operations, from the movement of the ladder to the direction of the nozzle, can be coordinated by a single firefighter standing on the turntable at the bottom of the ladder. If positioned correctly, an elevated master stream can pierce a raging inferno right to the seat of the fire and rapidly extinguish the blaze. But there is a risk. If positioned *poorly*, an elevated master stream can serve as a powerful tool for spreading a fire around an already burning structure by pushing the heat and gasses to areas of the building that are not already involved.

I knew the risk. In my mind, I had no choice. It had been fifteen minutes or more since I arrived at the scene and I had yet to get water on this fire. I called Ladder Three again, "How are we doing?"

"All clear, IC. We have the third floor evacuated, and the lower floors are clearing out."

Thank God, I silently prayed.

"Good work. Make sure everybody stays off the third floor. I'm starting master stream operations from the street."

I took a deep breath and made the order. Sixty seconds later Ladder Three's driver was hammering the fire from above, slamming thousands of gallons of precious water on the Centennial fire. Finally!

Meanwhile, like a stirred up ant hill, fire crews, chief officers, supply rigs, support personnel, and news media were all screaming toward the Centennial fire. One minute I was alone at my command post, and the next it was crawling with people.

Greg Keys in Battalion Three arrived first. Greg was an actual battalion chief, working in higher class as a division chief, and therefore the senior officer on scene. According to Austin protocols, chief officers always take command of an incident from a higher-class incident commander (captain acting as chief, like I was doing at the time). It's a smart protocol, and I agree with it. So, like the passing of a baton, I gave command to Greg, who then assigned me as his operations chief officer. The operations chief is tasked with coordinating all firefighting actions on the scene but has the flexibility to move around the incident rather than remain at the command post. The operations chief is the incident commander's eyes and ears on the scene. I took the job with a sigh of relief.

Next to arrive was my buddy James Ash, who made no apologies for his opinion of my strategy.

"What's up with the master streams, Kevin?" James asked with a furrowed brow.

"Can't get cut-off lines in place, James, and so far we have been consumed with search and rescue. I had to get some water on the fire. What do you suggest?"[14]

"I'll take the far corner on the southeast, sector two. We will get in from the rear if we have to cut a hole in the damn building. I'll get cut-off lines in place. Just keep that master stream off me and make sure somebody is doing the same thing from the other side." James stormed off to set up his sector, clearly angry about the absence of cut-off lines. Greg and I assigned the remaining sectors to various chiefs and acting chiefs and I headed out to supervise the cut-off effort.

The Centennial Condos looked like they had been fire-bombed. As I walked the length of the block headed to the rear of the structure, the sheer magnitude of the fire and the speed of its devastation awed me. In the center of the block, near the bridge of the H, the entire building had collapsed in on itself and was raging with fire. Blue plumes of fire, like welder's torches, were spewing and hissing—natural gas lines ruptured in the collapse now adding their two-cents to the already out-of-control blaze.

The vehicles on the street were all aflame, victims of radiant heat. Every three minutes or so a tire would explode, shaking the ground and rattling our already frayed nerves. Firefighters were all around placing equipment and dragging hose, working furiously to get lines into the rear of the structure. Saws were screaming as the firefighters cut their way into the rear.

And looking impassively down on all this devastation and activity were two magnificent firestorms, each hovering one hundred feet above the building, swirling and whirling like tornadoes of fire. To me they looked like the twin horns of the devil, arched at the top and growing in size as they met the roof of the building in a clash of noise and destruction. The sound was their laughter, I thought.[15]

This is your walk of shame, Rambo.

Fire raging through Sector Three of the Centennial Condominiums. Firefighters of Sector Three were making their stand inside the structure, just to the right of the picture. They were overwhelmed by the fire's unrelenting progress and retreated from the structure shortly after this picture was taken. Picture by Bob Parker, taken from the Kevin Baum library.

I quickly made my way to sector three on the southwest corner of the building, just opposite to and on the other side from sector two where James was preparing to make his stand.

The firefighters in sector three had cut through the barrier fence and were hastily advancing one-and-three-quarter-inch hand lines into the rear of the condominiums. There wasn't a whole lot of space for maneuvering behind the building—maybe six feet or so—so manipulating the rigidly charged lines through the gap and up the stairs was a massive challenge. I pulled some hose along and helped as much as I could while I jumped through the hole and ran up to the second floor to find my sector commander, but he was nowhere to be found. I finally rapped a captain on the helmet with my radio and asked him what the plan was.

"We're trying to get these cut-off lines in place, but every time we set up, the fire pushes right past us. It's kicking our butts, Chief, and I don't know how much longer we can last."

"If you don't last, sector two will be flanked by the fire as it wraps around the rear. What do you need to make your stand?"

"More hoses, water, and people," was his hasty reply. I told him they were on the way and to hang in there.

Now that I was inside the structure, I was easily able to move around within the building, and I wasted no time making the quick jog across the city block to sector two to check on James. I found him on the second floor, like a sentinel, standing rigidly erect, mask hanging from his face, chatting with Lieutenant Evans; both men were staring at the on-coming fire while they talked. If a look could extinguish fire, their gaze would have doused it in a second. As I approached them, Evans moved away and began to assemble the men of sector two into a small circle. I was about to ask James how it was going, but he put up a hand and motioned for me to watch. I looked over at Evans.

Harry Evans was a former Army Ranger and a no-nonsense officer known for his "damn-the-torpedoes" style. I used to joke about Harry having way too much starch in his boxers; he was just too militaristic for me. But you had to respect the guy. In fact, if I was stranded on a deserted island and I could pick one person to join me, it wouldn't be some sexy model, it would be Harry. Why? Because Harry would never give up until he was *off the island*. If you are going to be making a stand at the fire of your career, you want Harry to be there. I don't remember Harry's exact words that night as he motivated his men, but I do know it went something like this:

"Take a knee, men!" Harry screamed to the cluster of firefighters surrounding him, their helmets angled up, waiting for the speech.

"This is it, people!" he boomed.

"This is our Alamo! Only one thing stands between that fire and the complete loss of this building, and that is *you* and *me*. We're it! If we can't hold the line here, we lose everything. We have our lines in place. We have water. We can do this, but we have to work together. If the guys on the second floor give up, we put the guys on the third floor at risk. If the guys on the third floor lose ground, those of us down here are in danger. So *hold!*—*the!*—*line!* Don't retreat unless conditions are absolutely untenable; and, even then, go out fighting." Harry stared at his firefighters looking from one to another. "Questions? No? Then let's do this thing!"

The men screamed a hoorah and ran off to their lines. Harry grinned. I laughed. James stood like a proud father. Like almost everybody on the scene, Harry was working higher class that shift, but the difference was that Harry made it *look* classy.

Clearly sector two was in good hands. I wished James well and told him to call me if he needed anything and scooted back to sector three, which was rapidly losing its fight. In fact, sector three was a mess.

As I stood on the third floor and looked down onto the mayhem of the sector, I knew it was over. The west side of the building had seen the brunt of the collapse and the fire simply tore away at the building too quickly for the beleaguered firefighters. It was just a matter of time before the firefighters would be forced to retreat to the street to get out of harm's way. Once they were gone, there would be no stopping it, and it would be virtually impossible for James to fight the fire from two directions simultaneously, especially with operations on multiple floors.

I radioed Greg at the command post and gave him a status report. He acknowledged my report and ordered me back to the command post to assist with managing the ever-growing resource demands of the fire. I took one last look back at James and his crews, told the sector three officer to give it hell, and left the building for good. I would never see the inside of the Centennial Condominiums again because by the time it was all over there was no distinction between inside and out.

Seventy-five minutes after my arrival on the scene, the Austin Fire Department went defensive and pulled everybody out of the Centennial Condominiums. We had six alarms of firefighters and equipment on the scene—that's more than one hundred firefighters—but we still couldn't get ahead of that raging conflagration. I was standing outside of sector two when James and his men tumbled outside. Dirty, angry, and exhausted, the firefighters of sector two weren't ready to give up, but the time had come. James looked at me and scolded me, the decision, the entire department, and the world in a diatribe that best remains confidential. I didn't take it personally. He just didn't want to fail. Nobody did.

I was relieved on the scene just before noon on Saturday, December 14. My relief was a wide-eyed captain working in higher classification. As I jumped into the back of a pick-up truck that was shuttling firefighters to and from the stations for relief, I took one long last look at the burning pile of the once-proud complex. The images are only fragments in my mind, but here's what I remember seeing that morning: a complete city block of burning rubble billowing and puffing smoke amidst flare-ups of fire; master streams on every corner of the now missing structure pouring their futile streams onto the wreckage; weary firefighters everywhere too tired to swap war stories and too stunned to critique their actions; charred remains of vehicles, empty husks sitting on their rims, everything but the metal burned out; and finally, I remember seeing the shocked students looking on, all bundled up from the December cold, blood-shot eyes staring at what was once their home.

God, I thought, *did I make the right decisions last night? Is this my legacy?*

On the way back to the firehouse and pretty much every day since, I have consoled myself with this single thought:

Nobody died and no firefighters were injured.

I can live with that. [16]

Complete devastation of the Centennial Condominiums; an entire city block burned to the ground. The center section of the "H" is in the foreground, with the stairwell the only remaining standing structure. This is where Mike and his firefighters narrowly missed being buried in the collapse of the elevator car and housing. Picture by Bob Parker, taken from the Kevin Baum library.

LESSON FROM THE LINE
STRUCTURED EMPOWERMENT

> "You may never know what results come of your actions, but if you do nothing, there will be no result."
>
> Mahatma Gandhi

> "Don't be afraid to take a big step when one is indicated. You can't cross a chasm in two small steps."
>
> David Lloyd George

> "The function of leadership is to produce more leaders, not more followers."
>
> Ralph Nadar

There is probably no better job in the fire service than that of being the nozzleman at a working fire. Imagine a large garden hose with 100 to 120 pounds of pressure (per square inch) behind it, with a flow that is capable of filling a pool in minutes or a tub in seconds; a reach that can arc over a major highway; and an adjustable tip that allows you to manipulate your stream from a solid tube of rock-hard water to millions of tiny aerosolized droplets of showering H_2O. Now, imagine standing in front of a raging fire fully protected in your gear. You're breathing clean air through your pack, the heat isn't bad and you can take it, and on your side like a massive six-shooter rests your nozzle, awaiting your command. Like Clint Eastwood, you slowly pull up your weapon, square off with legs astride, aim your nozzle at the seat of the fire, and gently pull the valve open. As you do, the "tip reaction" pushes you back, back, back until you find solid footing as you lean at a thirty-degree angle into the pressure, using your body weight to control the line, which feels alive in your hands.[17] This is when you start smiling. "Make my day!" you scream, as you watch the fire rapidly evaporate in a steam explosion, hissing at you in a futile attempt to fight back. Slowly your legs begin to quiver from the stress, your arms begin to ache, your lower back is screaming at you, and your hands are going numb from hanging on to that nozzle, but you don't let go.

Your buddy behind you yells in your ear, "Take a break, I'll take the nozzle!"

You scream back, "No! I'm okay!"

He screams at you, "No, I really want to!"

You counter, "No I'm doing fine," as you make a mental note to ignore his next plea. But you're not fine. In fact, you're exhausted. But it doesn't matter; you are having the time of your life.

My first opportunity to be on the nozzle at a working fire was stolen from me by a lieutenant and I never forgave him for it. Nor did I forget what the experience taught me about giving up the nozzle.

We were at an apartment fire in east Austin. I was part of the first alarm compliment and arrived first on scene. The fire was on the exterior of the complex and was running up the siding and into the eaves. It looked impressive, as fire always does, but in reality it wasn't that big. My lieutenant told me to pull a "rack" line and hit the fire down low as quickly as possible and black it out.[18] He told me he would be there in a minute to lend a hand. I pulled my line, charged it, and was just about to open up on the fire when a lieutenant from Engine One, who had just arrived on the scene, jumped out of his rig, ran over, and shoved me aside (quite literally). "Gimme that!" he squealed and promptly took my nozzle and opened up on the fire. I didn't know what to do, and, as a rookie, I didn't have the courage to pile drive him headfirst into the mud, which is what I wanted to do.

I stood back to make sure it wasn't my lieutenant and then looked back at Engine One. His entire crew was standing there, doing nothing, watching him work the nozzle. No lines were being pulled, no supply lines were being set, no tools were coming off the rig. Just three blank stares. Their lieutenant hadn't given them any orders. He just jumped off and went to the first nozzle he saw.

I ran back to my lieutenant and found him helping the other firefighter set up a second line. "Why aren't you on that nozzle?" he scolded. I told him what had happened and he nodded that he understood. Slowly my lieutenant worked me up to the nozzle of our second line, and while I worked the nozzle he stood back and watched the progress, radio in hand and eyes on my stream. Every once in a while he would coach me along, advise me on stream pattern, show me where to hit the fire, ask me if I was tired, correct my actions if necessary, and help me move the hose. My lieutenant never once took the nozzle from me, and because he let me work the line I learned a lot about how to fight an exterior fire that day. The difference between these two lieutenants and their approach to their jobs was profound, and I have reflected on the events of that day many times as I slowly progressed through my career and tried to develop my own leadership style.

I share this short story with you as a prelude to our discussion on this chapter's lesson because it illustrates so well what I see happening in many organizations today.

Simply put, today it appears as if everybody wants to be "on the nozzle."

Leaders today don't want to *let go*; to truly empower their people; to stand back and change their perspective by giving their people the opportunity to experience new challenges; to grow professionally; to learn new things; to succeed or fail, whichever may be the case. In fact, I see just the opposite: employees being purposefully held back, "protected" from new opportunity and challenge or being told "That's not your responsibility" or "That's on a need-to-know basis and you don't need to know."

But in order to truly lead an organization and to grow new leaders, we have got to "give up the nozzle," stand back and change our perspectives, and really give our employees a chance to learn, grow, and contribute. Indeed, if everybody is "on the nozzle," who is truly in charge?

When the lieutenant from Engine One took the nozzle from me, embedded within his very actions was a coded message—one that was loud and clear to me at the time:

You can't do this, so I'll do it for you.

You're not important.

You're incompetent.

I don't trust you.

Go away.

Whether that was his message or not, it's certainly what I "heard."

What's more, look at what happened to his crew. The lieutenant's actions reduced them to bystanders; they were both frustrated and unproductive. If it hadn't been for my lieutenant and his leadership, I would have left that fire consumed with bitterness and resentment, feeling de-valued, unimportant, and powerless.

What message are you communicating to your employees today? What messages are embedded in your current practices, policies, and procedures? What are your employees "hearing" from you, your leaders, and your organization?

The Centennial Condominium fire represents, in my mind, *the* superlative example of a practice that appears to be unique to the fire service and what I have come to term "structured empowerment." We talk a lot today about "empowering" employees—or in the context of this lesson, "Giving up the nozzle"—and we see that word on plaques, in vision statements, on value propositions, and more. But we rarely see it woven into the very fabric of an organization's practices or structured into routine procedure. We all seem to appreciate the value of empowerment, but there appears to be wildly divergent opinions on *how* exactly to do it. Furthermore, I have discovered that many leaders like to talk the empowerment talk but in reality are not at all interested in letting go. They either will not or cannot "walk the walk."

In the fire service, we don't have any choice but to let go. Because of the unique demands of the emergency business, we have created, as a matter of necessity, a powerful tool for empowering, challenging, and growing the workforce, one that is structured into the very DNA of how the organization works. Of course I'm talking about the higher classification system.

At the Centennial fire, 90% of the officers and drivers on that scene were working in higher classification. Consider that carefully for a minute. This fire was one of, if not *the*, worst structure fire in the city's history. It was the career fire, the CNN fire, the Big One of the Big Ones, the signature local fire department event of the century. And yet, approximately 90% of the officers on the scene that night were out of their own assignment, forced to give up the nozzle and move into a new and challenging position and to tackle all the attendant responsibilities of this temporary promotion.

Now, imagine *the* signature event of your organization—whatever that might be, you decide. Got it in your head? Imagine that event occurring with a large percentage of your existing leadership or management gone.

What would be the outcome? Are you willing to trust your workforce with this heady responsibility?

I can imagine that today you would not want the signature event to occur in your organization without your core leadership present. But what if you had a process for structured empowerment in your organization and, because of it, everyone was cross-trained and prepared. Would you feel better? What if every member of your organization knew that on any given day he or she could be asked to step up into the supervisor's position and do his or her job for a day, a week, or a month. How do you think this knowledge would influence your employees' behavior and performance on a daily basis, including their willingness to learn more, take new risks, expand their perspectives, and seek opportunities to learn and grow? How do you think this knowledge would influence your supervisors' behavior toward their employees? How do you think this knowledge would influence overall organizational performance?

Higher classification is about *trust* and *letting go* (i.e., giving up the nozzle). Higher classification is not a sink-or-swim approach to delegation, but rather a form of structured empowerment that says to the workforce: "We will trust you to be prepared for increased responsibilities and we will train you to be ready. But when the time comes, *you* have to be willing to give up the nozzle, get out of your comfort zone, and take new risks and responsibilities. You can do it and we support you."

What an incredible message for employee and organizational development!

And while you can make the argument, and some have,

that the Centennial Condominium fire may have turned out differently if the existing leadership had been present that night, my counter to you would be simple: *How do you know?* What's more, how do you ever expect to grow new leaders if you don't give them a chance to succeed? Or to fail?

At the Centennial fire, nobody died and no firefighters were injured. I can live with that. Can you?

As you consider this lesson, remember this: Giving up the nozzle is scary, but in order to lead, and to lead well, we must teach our leaders to let it go.

TRADITION MATTERS

Of all the multiple assignments I had over the course of my twenty-one-year career with the Austin Fire Department, hands down my favorite was the three years I spent as a lieutenant in charge of Manpower Two.[19] The brain-child of then Austin Chief Bill Roberts, the manpower units represented a creative managerial approach to address the often conflicting demands between increasing necessary resources and simultaneously limiting costs to taxpayers. It is widely recognized in the fire service that fires are contained more quickly with less damage and less loss of life if we can get as many firefighters to the scene of a fire as quickly as possible. However, neither firefighters nor the equipment necessary for them to work are cheap.

Consider for a moment the cost of *just one* fire station. First, you have to build it; if you build a fire station to today's standards, depending on impervious cover requirements and other local code issues, you are looking at anywhere from 3 to 8 million dollars, frequently much more. So, for the purposes of this example, let's agree on $5 million. You then have to equip that station with state-of-the art apparatus and equipment—another $1.5

million, roughly. Now, staff that station with five firefighters per shift, or fifteen full-time employees. After pay and benefits, let's place a conservative price on the firefighters at $50,000 each, bringing us to $750,000 per year for the crews, which does not include the price to train them. This brings the total cost just to open a new fire station to roughly *$7.25 million*. I don't care what part of the country you live in, by any standard, that's a lot.

So, how do you increase the number of firefighters you have on the streets without all the costs associated with building new fire stations and purchasing expensive red fire trucks? You simply assign four firefighters to an existing station, buy a sport utility vehicle and park it next to the existing rig, put only personal protective equipment in the back of the wagon, call it a manpower unit, and give the crew one of the most coveted jobs in the fire service—responding to *all* fires in the city as a resource pool. Now your only expenses are the SUV and the firefighters, a savings of millions of dollars to your taxpayers while simultaneously improving your ability to deliver service. Pretty clever.

But you're probably thinking: *Wait, what about firefighting equipment?* Good question. Every firefighting rig on the planet, if properly equipped, carries more firefighting equipment than the assigned crew will typically use at an emergency incident. As I already mentioned, the fire service is wisely built upon a model of redundancy. At any major emergency incident, with all those fire trucks on scene, you will always have more than enough equipment to support not only your own crew, but also that of many others. This redundancy is necessary because only a small percent of the firefighting apparatus on a scene will actually be positioned close to the incident. Due to limitations in street size, traffic congestion, building configurations, hose line placement, apparatus size, and other factors, fire crews frequently have to park their rigs blocks from an actual emergency. However, firefighters on an emergency scene need to be able to grab equipment quickly at an evolving incident without having to run blocks to where their rigs are parked. Speed is always the priority, hence the equipment redundancy. Since manpower units were designed almost exclusively as a human resource pool for fires and major incidents, it was assumed, quite correctly, that there would be ample equipment for the crew to commandeer on a scene; which is exactly what we did.

Chief Roberts commissioned three manpower units and positioned them north, central, and south. Named after the corresponding station to which they were each assigned, everybody wanted to be on the centrally located Manpower Two. Why? Because Station Two, and hence the centrally located manpower unit, had easy access to all major roads and highways, and thus the speed with which it could arrive anywhere in the city made Manpower Two the single most active firefighting unit in the city, bar none. A firefighter riding on Manpower Two could expect to fight more fires in a single year than many firefighters would see in an entire career. Talk about hands-on experience.

I was awarded the command of Manpower Two after I completed a three-year staff tour as the department's public information officer. I was replacing a strong lieutenant with a reputation for brass-tacks firefighting. He had staffed his rig with some of the finest firefighters I had ever worked with. These firefighters were naturally skeptical about their green lieutenant who had just finished a three-year rotation in a non-combat assignment. In fact, I'll never forget my first run with these guys. It was a high-rise box alarm downtown—smoke in a corridor. We arrived on scene and before I could get my wits about me all three of my men were fully bunkered out, breathing apparatus on their backs and gear in their hands. They took one look at me while I was fumbling with my jacket couplings, shook their heads, and started jogging toward the fire. "Catch up if you can, LT," said my driver, and off they went. When we later returned to the unit, with the appropriate level of humility in my voice, I informed my crew that in the future I would prefer that they *not* leave their officer behind—it was a matter of company integrity and all that.

A firefighter named Mark Fleischauer, who was nicknamed Flyswatter, replied, "Well, maybe you better practice getting your gear on faster, LT."

The crew of Manpower Two on the B shift took great pride in its firefighting reputation and made it very clear to me that I would either conform to its standards or be left in the dust. I conformed.

Housing both the manpower unit and Engine Two, Station Two is located just west of the University of Texas campus and stands as an anachronism in an area gone modern. The second fire station commissioned into service in the city of Austin[20] and built in the late 1800s, Station Two looks more like a gasthaus plucked right out of Heidelberg, Germany, than a fire station serving one of America's most cosmopolitan cities. Station Two today is surrounded by modern apartment complexes, high-rise dormitories and strip shopping centers and is almost right in the center of downtown Austin. Standing watch over the modern landscape, Station Two represents in many ways a time capsule into fire service heritage and tradition. In fact, it didn't matter how many long years I was assigned there, working at Station Two, to me, was akin to walking an old battlefield or exploring an ancient graveyard—you just couldn't *help* but experience a feeling of history and a sense of belonging to a profession that has profoundly deep roots. Every shift we kept company with the ghosts of firefighters who had long since past, hearing the echoes of the hooves of the horses that grazed the bays, ready to pull the old steam engines if the bell rang. If only the walls could talk, what stories they would tell.

A brick-and-mortar building with beautiful lines, Station Two is a two-story, "pole-hole" house. Back in the early days of the fire service, we used to build our fire stations with two primary practical considerations—sleeping quarters for the firefighters and bay rooms for the horses and rigs. In order to save space, older stations were "stacked," with the dormitories and living space located directly above the truck bays. To save time in an emergency, these stacked stations were equipped with three-inch poles that the firefighters could slide on from dorm to bay, collapsing the amount of time it took to mobilize a sleeping crew into action, hence the name "pole-hole" station. Station Two had a single pole that landed in the middle of the truck bay.

When you stand on the street and look at a two-story pole-holer, such as Station Two, what strikes you immediately is the height of the building. It just seems to be too tall for a two-story house. The reason for this strange appearance is the presence of hay lofts between the two floors. In order to keep the hay close and dry for the horses, firefighters used to store hay and feed in the truck-room lofts. Firefighters could simply grab a pitchfork, scoop out some hay, throw it on the floor, and feed the stock. Station Two had several of these lofts in the truck-room ceiling. Climb up into one of these hay lofts today and you can still smell the musty order of horses and feed.

Station Two B shift was a bizarre melting pot of personalities, which is what kept it interesting and made working there so much fun. You never knew what each day might bring at Station Two, and I absolutely loved going to work in anticipation of the shift's activity. Indeed, on my unit alone rode three firefighters whose personality differences prescribed a daily and always hilarious clash of wits, humor, and bantering. My driver was a massive man named Mike Bewley. At six foot, four inches tall, with a football player's frame, Mike was a well-educated, fast-talking Hispanic with an abundance of testosterone. Even though Mike was a great firefighter—, Mike was quite famous within the department for the speed with which he could tear down a wall—his real passion was politics; in fact, he had served on a number of campaigns prior to joining the department. According to Mike, everything was political, and it was impossible to have a conversation without him somehow turning it to politics. The crew used to scream at him to shut up, but Mike would just keep on ranting about politics.

On the back of the manpower rode two firefighters: Mark "Flyswatter" Fleischauer and Rob Horne. Mark was a power nerd. He was the guy who would read a book about computer programming and then turn around, buy a computer and make it do incredible things, and tell us all about it, regardless of our interest (or lack thereof). Mark was our go-to guy for just about any problem we couldn't solve. Indeed, there were very few things Mark could not do or would not try, and there was an element of genius in his nerdy creativity. Of the many talents that Mark possessed, he was particularly well known for his welding skills. Most of the downtown station basketball hoops were welded by Mark, and he was the creator of a powerfully effective forcible-entry tool called the "Dragon Slayer." With a massive saw on one end and a hook on the other, the Dragon Slayer, in the right hands, could be a formidable tool for destroying just about anything. And those hands usually belonged to Mike, who would show up at shift change and scream, "Where's my Dragon Slayer? Where's my Dragon Slayer?!" Once he found it, Mike would pet the Dragon Slayer and talk to it: "You and me, we're a team, baby. Don't ever leave me like that again. I need you as much as you need me." Mike would purr as he caressed the tool, while the rest of us would just look on and laugh.

On the other side was Rob Horne. Rob was young, handsome, quiet, fiercely intelligent, and fastidious with, well, everything. Rob was the guy who would compartmentalize, label, and regularly dust his wall locker, food locker, bunker locker, and whatever else he used to organize his life. If you forgot a pair of socks, you always knew that Rob had a few extra pairs, right there in the slot labeled "Socks." But don't bother asking; he wouldn't loan you a pair because sharing socks is not healthy from a hygienic perspective, and you should have remembered to bring your own socks anyway. Rob ate only the healthiest of foods, exercised like a professional athlete, controlled his temper and opinions, never deviated from safety protocols, and spent the majority of a shift reading books about medicine. Mike used to taunt Rob with temptation, "C'mon, Rob, you can eat grease like the rest of us. Only the good die young, man!" But Rob wouldn't waver. Whatever you thought of his proclivities, Rob's discipline commanded respect, and I was glad to have him on my rig.

That was my crew, and they made life interesting.

When I reflect on the good days at Station Two, while my mind is full of fond memories, one shift stands out in particular.

We were running the Pony Express for headquarters on a late summer afternoon. In the fire service, since you have so many different work sites distributed across the city (and over three shifts), communication can be quite difficult. In the pre-Internet and e-mail days, we used to run a weekly Pony Express. The "Pony" was nothing more than an interoffice mail delivery system—a way to distribute timely information, materials, and resources across the organization. Since the manpower units had a city-wide response territory, we were frequently called upon to deliver the Pony for the department. My guys used to hate the assignment, especially Mike, who would rant on and on about using some of the best firefighters in the department as delivery boys, but I enjoyed the task. It was an opportunity to see guys who I had not seen in years, share a cup of coffee, and get to know new people. It was also fun to listen to my crew chatter on about who knows what as we drove around the city.

A typical conversation in Manpower Two went something like this:

"Dude, you are so full of it." Mike to Mark. "It's indisputable that the reason the wall fell is because of internal issues independent of the arms race. Reagan didn't do it. That's BS."

"No, Mike, you're wrong. Again. It's because of Reagan and the massive amount of money he put into the arms race that the Russians had to spend so much money to keep up, which broke the bank, ultimately resulting in the fall of the empire."

"Empire? Empire!? We're not talking about Star Wars here, Goofy. Who are you, Luke Skywalker? What are you talking about, Fly? Rob, get into this."

Rob: "I don't think it's appropriate to talk politics at work."

Mike: "Rob, you're a wimp."

Rob: "Perhaps, but you're a bully."

Mark: "And ugly, like Chewbacca."

"How did I get assigned to this crew?" Mike moaned.

Me: "All of you, shut up. I think we're about to get a call."

During the debate on the fall of the Soviet Union, I had been listening to the radio, monitoring a north-Austin brushfire that seemed to be getting out of control. Just as I hushed my crew, I heard the officer on scene call dispatch and order a full Brush Alarm. His voice was high and quick, meaning that he was probably up against a real challenge.

"Let's go, Mike," I said as I called dispatch and confirmed our response to the fire.

"Heehaw!" Mike hooted. He hit the lights and sirens and merged into the left lane of traffic. "Manpower Two is on the case!"

Emergency response is dangerous. Have a look at the data on firefighter injuries and fatalities and you will quickly notice that the very act of responding to a fire or an emergency can kill a person. The fire service has recognized this hazard and made a number of improvements in both technology and protocol in order to protect firefighters (and civilians) during the response phase of an incident. Chief among the technology improvements has been the rigs themselves.

When I first got into the fire department, firefighters were still riding on the tailboard of the pumpers as they responded to an emergency; this is why, not surprisingly, we still refer to rookies today as "Tailboardmen."[21] But, as you can probably imagine, riding back there was terribly dangerous. Today, both fire pumpers and hook-and-ladder trucks have enclosed cabs for all responding firefighters to sit in. Everybody is inside, buckled up, connected via intercom, and safe.

Technology is a double-edged sword, however. The very same technology—enclosing cabs into airtight compartments—has made modern vehicles, such as your sedan parked out front, so insulated that you can't even hear a fire truck as it approaches behind you. Turn on your air conditioner and radio while sitting in your airtight Cadillac and you can literally be right in front of a fire truck with lights and sirens blaring and not hear it. This has led to even more accidents, which has motivated changes in policy.

Chief among these policy changes has been to *slow down*. Today most large cities do not allow their fire trucks to respond more than 10 mph over the posted speed limit. To go any faster just gets too dangerous. We used to blow right through a red light in the old days, comforted that our entire racket had alerted motorists of our impending approach. Today, you can't count on the noise, so we stop before we go through intersections and slow down considerably on congested roads. Even though speed is of utmost importance, if you don't get there at all, then what good are you? It makes more sense to go slowly and get there safely.

However, getting Mike to slow down was a constant challenge.

We were merging onto the major north-south artery in west Austin to make a quick sprint up the highway to the fire when I heard Mike spew a litany of curse words. I looked up from my map to see the object of his complaint. Just in front of us on the highway was Unit 102, the safety chief's vehicle, running code three to the same brushfire

Lessons from the Line · 135

as Manpower Two. Driving the rig was the safety officer, a battalion chief, and in the rig with him was the fire chief and the B-shift division chief—essentially the core leadership of the entire department for the shift.

"What twisted timing is that!" raged Mike.

"Ease in behind him, Mike, and give him breathing room. You know the rules," I said, referring to the department's unequivocal policy related to passing other emergency vehicles. During emergency response, when you find yourself "merging" with another responding vehicle, according to policy you must give right of way to the leading rig and then stay behind it for the duration of the ride. Only in rare cases do you ever pass another vehicle, and even then there is a laundry list of radio procedures that have to take place before the pass can occur.

"Let me go around him, LT," stormed Mike. "Look at this! He's going the speed limit! We're being passed by other vehicles!" Mike was beside himself, pounding the steering wheel in his anger.

"This *is* kind of embarrassing," joined Mark. "What's their problem up there?"

Even the ever-neutral Rob had to opine, "Are we even going the speed limit? Sure feels slow back here."

It *was* frustrating. Here we were, running Code Three on the highway en route to a working brushfire with firefighters on the scene calling for help, and we were getting passed by civilian vehicles on the highway, drivers looking at us with bemused expressions and kids waving bye as they sped past. My crew and I were seasoned firefighters, anxious to get to the scene and lend a hand. These guys up front just wanted to get to the fire to watch—high-brass rubbernecking.

"It's almost like they are slowing down just to jack with us, LT. Come on, let's go around him!"

"We don't have any hair on our ass if we don't pass them," Mark said flatly. Not a challenge, just an observation.

That's when I made a bad decision. "Okay, Mike, let's take him. But I want you to wait for a large opening in the traffic, go all the way to the right so that he can clearly see you, and then pass him *slowly*."

Mike only heard the "pass him" part and zoomed right on by; as he did, Mike smiled and waved and let fly a comment that doesn't belong in this book.

We never made it to the fire. We were promptly canceled and told to report immediately to quarters at Station Two. On the way back I had plenty of time to muse over my impending fate. It wouldn't be completely accurate to say that my life flashed before my eyes, but I knew one thing for sure: I was scared and absolutely certain that I was about to find myself surrounded by raging bugles.

The bugle is probably one of the most recognized symbols of fire service tradition and heritage. In fact, visit your local fire department and I'll wager that you will see them everywhere—on the walls, on shelves, in pictures, and on the lapels of officers. Back in the early days of the fire service, long before radios and modern apparatus were invented, fire company officers were constantly vexed by their inability to communicate with each other and their men while working on scene. To address this problem, fire officers began the practice of carrying large horns, or bugles, similar to what you see cheerleaders using at a college football game.

The officers used these bugles like megaphones and would shout orders to their crews through the bugles and, in so doing, improve scene coordination between fire companies. You could always tell who was in charge of a fire back in those days because he would be out on the street, commanding the fire, and ordering his troops through a large bugle. If a bystander or reporter showed up on scene and asked, "Who is in charge?" a firefighter would simply reply, "Look for the guy with the bugles."

Today the bugle is the symbol of fire service leadership and denotes an officer's rank within the department. Lieutenants wear one bugle on their lapel; captains have two in a cross; battalion chiefs have three in a cluster; division chiefs have four in a cluster; assistant fire chiefs have five in a cluster; and fire chiefs have six bugles in a magnificent round cluster of authority. Want to find out who is in charge of a fire department? Look for the guy or gal with all the bugles.

When we returned to quarters at Station Two, the crew of Engine Two was in the middle of a station tour. Since Station Two is so rich with history and tradition, it is a popular place for school kids and other citizens groups to visit. And, since a fire department considers itself to be a part of the community it serves, the door is always open to anybody that wants to come in and visit to learn more about the profession and the people who live it.[22] We had tours regularly, but at the time I wasn't in the mood for a crowd.

Jim Eberle, the lieutenant in charge of Engine Two

and one of the finest men I have ever had the pleasure to call friend, approached me with a grin.

"What the *hell* did you do out there, Kevin?" I told him the story.

"Well, brace yourself. The fire chief's office just called and you have been summoned to HQ immediately. They only want you and Mike. I'll take Rob and Fly on the Engine."

"*The* chief?"

"*The* chief," Jim said somberly.

I groaned. Jim patted me on the back and said with a grin, "We'll be there with you—in spirit."

"Thanks," was my only reply.

Thirty minutes later Mike and I were ushered into the fire chief's office.

The fire chief had a monstrous oval conference table in his office, one that I had seen numerous times before in my role as public information officer. I always thought the table was out of place—a gross statement of over-indulgence and a bit extravagant for a chief's office. But today all I noticed was that every seat but two was occupied by a guy wearing a white shirt sporting clusters of bugles on his lapel. There were six chief officers sitting around that table, waiting on poor Mike and me to take a seat. Mike later commented that there were enough bugles sitting at that table to start a symphony. My heart was in my throat as the fire chief started his rant, eyes burning holes into my brain.

"You passed the wrong vehicle today, son!"

This is not starting well, I thought.

"I have no idea what you were thinking out there; in

fact, I'm quite sure you *were not* thinking! Don't you know the protocols for passing? I know you do, don't say you don't. This is serious! Very serious! What am I to do with you? You blatantly pass the safety chief's vehicle—the *safety chief's* vehicle!—and then zoom on by like you have no care in the world. What's more," and he leveled a finger at Mike, "*You* are *smiling* at us while you do it like it's a Sunday drive to the park! You two leave me no choice; this has to be dealt with swiftly and harshly. What do you have to say for yourself, Lieutenant Baum?!"

It was more accusation than question.

Mike started to open his mouth in reply but I quickly hushed him. As I sat there thinking of a response, not knowing what I should say, I remembered the wise advice my grandfather once gave me: *Kevin, always remember, when you make a mistake, admit it. There is great nobility in owning up to our mistakes.* I said a quick prayer to my grandfather, swallowed deeply, and opened my mouth:

"Chief, I apologize. I am the officer of Manpower Two and I made the decision to pass your vehicle. I know the protocols and I knowingly violated them. If anybody is going to get in trouble—and I agree with you that somebody should—let it be me and not my crew. They were just doing their jobs. I am ultimately responsible and I made the decision and I accept full responsibility. I regret the decision but know that I can't take it back. At the time I thought it would be safe, but hindsight tells a different story. I can tell you it will never happen again. With that said, I will now accept whatever punishment you feel is appropriate because I've earned it."

As I spoke I lifted both my hands to the table and by the time I was finished I had them on the table, palms up, and wrists locked, symbolically ready for the cuffs. My mouth was dry as a bone and I was literally shaking under the table from nerves, but I really saw no other alternative.

And then the miracle happened. All the chief officers around that table simply sat there, mouths and eyes wide open, speechless. I have no idea what they expected out of me, but I know it wasn't what they got. It was obvious that they truly didn't know what to say. My words apparently knocked them off balance. We all just sat there looking at each other for the longest two minutes of my life. Finally, the fire chief changed his expression and said softly, "Well, sounds like you regret the decision and are willing to own it. That's all I can ask from my officers. Don't let it happen again, Lieutenant Baum. You're excused."

And that was that.

Back in the manpower, Mike kept asking me to pinch him to make sure we were still alive. Neither one of us could believe we were not put off without pay, one of the most severe punishments firefighters face, or transferred or worse. I felt as if we had been given a once-in-a-lifetime reprieve with a caveat that we should learn from the experience. I said as much to Mike during the ride home. "There's an obvious lesson in this for us, Mike. I think we should heed its advice."

Mike looked at me for a long moment and then finally agreed, "Perhaps you're right. Next time we won't pass them at all. We'll just take an exit and haul ass on a different route using the back roads as cover." I rolled my eyes and we both laughed.

Lessons from the Line

Right as we pulled into the fire station, Mike mentioned the obvious. "You know, LT, we are going to get wormed mercilessly over this." I acknowledged that it was indeed going to be painful as we both jumped out of the rig and went into the fire station to face the music.

A long-standing fire service tradition is an act called "worming." It is difficult to describe exactly, or to define with any degree of clarity what is meant by the term "worm" in the fire service. All firefighters know perfectly well what worm means until somebody asks them to explain it. And to make matters more difficult, like so many words in the English language, worm can mean several different things depending upon the context within which it is used.

In the simplest terms, a worm is a practical joke, but it goes much, much deeper than that. Worming is really a fundamental part of fire service culture—a long-standing practice of good-natured give and take between professionals that serves multiple purposes. For example, if a rookie is falling short of expectations, peer firefighters will worm him until he shapes up. The worm can take several forms, such as sneaking flour into his sheets so that he wakes up covered in white powder or identifying his emotional soft spot and tenaciously picking at it. In this case, the worm is a subtle form of social pressure or a cultural corrective device.

A worm can also be something that happened to you or your crew, usually something embarrassing. For example, if a firefighter is on a traffic accident and swipes his finger in fluid under a car (ostensibly checking for a hydrocarbon leak), only to find out as he smells it that the fluid is really just the byproduct of a nervous driver's bowels, that firefighter just wormed himself and gave his peers great fodder for future worms directed toward him.[23] Indeed, the self-inflicted worms are almost always the best.

One of the most famous Austin Fire Department self-inflicted worms, and my favorite, was earned by a crew at Fire Station Nineteen back in the late 70s. One of the firefighters was out front cleaning the rig when a "wild" chicken strutted up. He grabbed the chicken and took it inside, initiating what must have been a fascinating debate between the firefighters about what to do with the chicken. Finally, it was decided that the only noble thing to do would be to eat it, which is exactly what they did. Chicken stew, I think. A couple of hours later, after the meal, a cute little girl came by the station with tears in her eyes and asked if the firefighters had seen her pet chicken, which had been missing for some time. With plates full of chicken bones and full stomachs, the firefighters stood before her speechless, thoroughly wormed by the turn of events.[24]

While it may seem strange to an outsider, a worm is, in many ways, the red thread that ties together and bonds firefighters into a social and professional family. Worms become the folklore that gives personality to the profession. The worm represents a good-natured statement that says, "You are accepted and part of the family, therefore go forth and expect to be joked along the way." Worming, over time, becomes hardwired into the firefighter's very psyche and is the universal translator that says, "You are one of us."

As we pulled into the station, Mike was simply saying what we both already knew: we had thoroughly wormed ourselves by passing the chief's car, and we could expect no quarter in the response from our peers. We were right, of course.

They were all waiting for us at the kitchen table. Word had already gotten around in the short time it took us to drive home that we had narrowly escaped the guillotine and had received a get-out-of-jail-free pass. Together we all sat around the table while Mike and I told the story.

The guys were shocked that we had escaped unscathed and we were laughing and hooting as the story was told again and again. That's when the worming started in earnest. New nicknames, such as "Chief-Wormers" and "White Cats," were ascribed to Mike and me. We received phone calls from other stations asking for advice on how to pass a chief and stay alive. Homemade placards taped to the side of the manpower wagon stating, "Where Chiefs Dare to Tread!" or "Pass with Care" were affixed to the rig. Finally, the guys pulled Mike and me into the day room, where Fly had drawn a magnificent wall portrait on the chalkboard. In character on the board, in color, was Manpower Two bouncing along the highway full throttle, throwing dust in its trail. There was an arm stuck outside each of the four windows, representing myself and the crew (I suppose), and every middle finger was outstretched in the universal symbol of, well, you get the picture. There were bubble captions for each firefighter stating various words to the chiefs, who were under the wheels getting run over. It was a masterpiece—one that they must have started the moment we left the station to meet the chief. It was so good that other crews from nearby stations stopped by to admire the work. Like artisans staring at the *Mona Lisa* in the Louvre, they would stand back and admire the masterpiece, occasionally picking up a stick of chalk and adding their two cents to the worm.

Jim Eberle declared that our good fortune warranted a "wagon," and Mike and I had no choice but to capitulate.

A "wagon," in the fire service, is essentially a meal or ice cream or anything that a firefighter can eat that is a reward for somebody else's good fortune. Some fire stations have wagons that are standing rituals, meaning that every shift they eat together, either taking turns to cook for each other or, more likely, paying to have the station's best cook prepare the meals for them. These "standing wagons" can be literal feasts, depending on the fire station, with freshly baked bread, salads, meat, potatoes, vegetables, and desserts.

A wagon is also a celebration. Any time something good happens to a firefighter, such as a birthday, a promotion, or, as in this case, surviving a stupid decision (mine), it's tradition for the honored firefighter to cook for his station buddies. The expectation for the size of the wagon is directly associated with the significance of the event. For example, ice cream and home-baked cakes are perfectly appropriate for a birthday, since we all have them and they come around every year. So, depending on how many firefighters you have assigned to a station, you know you are going to get that number of cakes and cookies over the course of a typical year. It's a pretty good perk to the job.

Since a promotion is a big deal because it happens rarely, the expectation for this event is that the firefighter being promoted will cook a full meal for his pals. Nothing is worse than to cook short for an important wagon, meaning either you didn't cook enough food or, worse yet, your choice in cuisine is not appropriate to the occasion, such as preparing a simple spaghetti meal for a promotion to chief officer, a promotion that *must* receive the honor of surf and turf.

For the wagon, Mike and I decided on steaks. After all, you only pass a chief once in a career and live to tell about it! Together, the crews of Station Two dined that night on the finest the butcher had to offer while Mike and I obeyed the rules of tradition and doted on our peers as servants to royalty. Even Rob splurged and ate a steak that night.

A few months later, I was saying goodbye to my comrades and friends at Fire Station Two. The department had changed fire chiefs and word had come down that the new chief planned to decommission the manpowers. An administrator with extremely limited combat experience, the new chief just didn't see the value in the mission. I tried to influence the decision as best I could and even went so far as to write a position paper on the value of the manpowers, but the chief's mind was already made up. He made his decision without even consulting with the officers of the three manpower units, an oversight that I never forgot.[25] In a fit of frustration, I decided to "retaliate" by throwing myself into the books for a captain's promotion.

My philosophy was then and still is today that if you don't like a decision, don't complain about it; rather, do everything you can to put yourself in a position so that next time, *you* are the one making the decisions. Even though I was angry with the chief and his decision at the time, in hindsight, it was the decommissioning of the manpowers that began the chain reaction that would cause me to one day become a fire chief myself. Had that decision not been made, it is very likely I would still be a lieutenant on Manpower Two today. Such are the twists of fate.

My efforts were rewarded with a promotion to captain a few months later.

My last shift at Station Two was pretty much like the hundreds that came before it. Jim and I spent some quiet time in the officer's dorm reliving experiences, like the time the rookie got stuck in the pole hole, squealing like a pig, while Rob, in a fit of exasperation because he couldn't get him out, flatly said, "Let's just leave him there. He's not going anywhere." And the time that the fire engine "drove" out of the station on its own because the driver forgot to set the brake. We laughed together, water in our eyes, bellies full of my steak wagon, cups of fresh black coffee hot in our hands, reliving worm after worm after worm. I miss Jim. I miss all my Station Two buddies.

Just before shift change I called my wife and told her to swing by and pick me up. We were headed to the lake to celebrate my promotion, but also, I needed her to help me escape the water bath that I knew was coming. It's tradition in the fire service to worm a promoting peer on his last shift at the station. This worm can take many forms, but usually it's a water bath of some sort. I have seen the most ingenious contraptions for covertly trapping a firefighter in a bath of water: from buckets suspended from the ceiling with a remote trigger, to power guns hidden in the walls, to firefighters on the roof. I knew it was coming and I was taking great pride in the fact that I had so far thwarted a really good soaking. I figured if I had my wife pick me up, I could discourage them from soaking me as I got into her car.

As I was saying my goodbyes, you could tell the guys were up to something. They were sheepish and giggly. Mark and Rob hugged me first and then headed out to the truck room as I started to make the rounds. As I did so, I remember looking at the station—the hay loft doors, the pole, the architecture, the soon-to-be-decommissioned Manpower, the rustic old décor—thinking how gifted I had been to work in such a historic building, so rich in fire service heritage and with such a great group of guys. I knew I would miss all of it.

At last, standing toe to toe with my good friend Jim Eberle, I said, "Well, I think I will miss you the most, Scarecrow." Jim smiled, looked me in the eyes, and gave me a big bear hug. We promised to keep in touch, but we both knew it would not be the same. It never is.

I turned on a heel and snuck out the back door, fully expecting a dousing of water. Nothing happened. I could see my wife parked at the end of the alley just next to the station out front. Nobody was in sight. *Ah, well,* I thought, *looks like I'm in the clear.* As I rounded the corner and began a slow jog to the car, they hit me. Mark and Rob were out front manning a one-and-a-half-inch hose line, charged by Engine Two, poised and ready to open the nozzle as soon as I appeared, which I did right on cue. They soaked me to the bone and sent me spinning in the mist.

With a huge smile on my face, I slithered through the roaring spray to my wife's car and jumped in. "Get outta here, baby!" I screamed, as tears rolled down my cheeks. Gwen looked at me, saw the tears, and asked, "Are you sad, Kev?" I stared out the windshield as we drove through the mist and just smiled back.

I would not see the entire crew of Station Two B shift in the same place at the same time for another seven years—when we met to honor a fallen Station Two brother.

LESSON FROM THE LINE
COMMUNITY & FELLOWSHIP

"Tradition is a guide, not a jailer."

William Somerset Maugham

"A tradition without intelligence is not worth having."

T.S. Eliot

"If you don't stand for something, you'll fall for anything."

Ancient Proverb

I recently had the opportunity to work with a large West Coast organization that was experiencing severe problems with employee retention. The organization was, and still is, under terrific management with a team of strong and caring leaders at the helm. This team of leaders was deeply concerned with its turnover rate as the organization was losing, on average, nearly 50% of its new hires within the first two years of employment, meaning one of every two new hires would be *gone* within two years. Besides the obvious issues created by high turnover, this phenomenon was even more problematic due to the lost investment the organization suffered every time a new hire walked out the door. It cost tens of thousands of dollars just to train each employee before he or she could even begin to meaningfully contribute to the organization. When employees walked out, they took the investment *and* the skills with them. To make matters worse, almost 60% of the organization's *total* workforce was eligible for retirement, and many of them had announced that they would retire in five years or less. If everybody that was eligible for retirement decided to leave at once, the organization would be crippled; indeed, it would fail.

My client asked me to conduct a series of focus groups with the employees and stakeholders in an effort to identify the cause of the high turnover and then to develop possible intervention strategies to turn it around. The employee groups came up with a number of intriguing ideas on the cause of the turnover: long and unappealing commutes to work; long work hours with mandatory overtime; high West Coast cost of living; a competitive job market with lots of alternate opportunities; and more. However, I still felt that we were missing the root cause of the problem and skirting the real issues.

That's when I started to ask the following questions:
"How does your organization define itself?"
"What is your corporate identity?"

"What rituals, norms, symbols, artifacts, and traditions give meaning to your profession?"

"Do you have a corporate folklore—the stories that give a historical meaning to your profession?"

"What is it about your job and career that gives you a sense of fellowship and belonging?"

Their answers were shocking! Without going into great detail, suffice to say that there was no apparent corporate identity and no agreed-upon set of traditions that defined their profession. The only consensus we could find was that economy and efficiency were the rules of the day. Do more with less. Increase the bottom line. Work harder and work more. The employees did not feel that they were part of a unique profession and there was a clear lack of fellowship and a sense of belonging to something larger than themselves. In fact, quite the opposite was true: the organization was suffering from an "every man for himself" culture. Take care of number one and let the rest fight for themselves.

And they wonder why turnover is high? I'm convinced that this organization's turnover problem is not due to a series of external variables, such as long commutes or mandatory overtime, but rather because there are no *internal* forces binding the new hires to the organization. The employees do not feel they are a part of a broader purpose, a community, a family, or a rich heritage. Their work simply lacks meaning beyond the work itself, which makes it easy to walk away.

If you doubt this example, swallow hard and take a look

around you. I believe their story is boilerplate for most large organizations today. Indeed, I see it everywhere.

Here's what I think is happening. If the management scholars seem to agree on anything today, it is that change is the one constant we can expect in organizational life. "The Internet and other "flattening" technologies will continue to increase trends toward globalization, ratcheting up competition," they argue. "And the only organizations that will survive in today's changing world are those that become nimble, flexible, adaptable, diverse, and quick in reflex to shifting market demands."

The scholars make a good point, and they are right. However, while the obsession with creating nimble organizations in an increasingly "flat" and high-tech world is important, I believe this mandate is incomplete. Today we should be focusing on and creating not just nimble organizations that are flexible and adaptable to change, but on creating nimble organizations that are both flexible and adaptable while simultaneously anchored to a broader set of traditions that gives the organization its identity, meaning, stability, and form.

Unfortunately, what I see all too often today is a form of corporate identity crisis—a wavering, fuzzy, and incomplete understanding of *who* a company or an agency is as an organization. Organizations and their leaders today seem to be so focused on change that this very obsession creates, over time, an organization that is *itself* always changing, rootless, and rudderless. This fuzziness has powerful implications on organizational performance and employee productivity. However, I do not think this organizational schizophrenia is due to an absence of defining qualities—traditions, symbols, artifacts, and rituals. Rather, I think we have become so obsessed with competition, economy, and efficiency (getting the work done!), that we have simply lost sight of our collective organizational identity. We have pushed it to the side because, well, we're busy.

But at what cost?

Tradition has received a bad rap over the years. Tradition is lamented today as the single greatest obstacle to change. In many cases, tradition has earned its bad rap because it can serve as a powerful force to slow growth and stunt an organization. I recently watched a television interview of a Hewlett Packard executive who complained that the HP Way today is the wrong way. She argued that the company's obsession with the HP Way tradition had actually become an obstacle to change and, because of it, the organization was falling behind its competitors (this may or may not be the case, but it was an interesting interview nonetheless).

When I say that tradition matters, I'm not referring to old dogmas or outdated technologies. And I'm definitely not extolling that curmudgeonly old fart that tells you, "That ain't the way we do business around here, young feller." What I am saying is that organizations today can learn from the Firefighter Model when it comes to balancing tradition with growth and in the process maintain a healthy, professional organizational identity.

Think about Station Two for a minute. Here is a historic building with all the artifacts and heritage that come with it. But parked right inside of that old and historic building is the most modern fire apparatus money can buy.

That fire engine has more technological bells and whistles than most small airplanes. It has a computer system in the officer's compartment, remote controls, foam inductors for fighting hydrocarbon fires, and much, much more. And yet it is surrounded by history and tradition; indeed, just above it rest the old hay lofts. What a compelling juxtaposition—a merger and collaboration between the modern and the traditional. And inside of that fire station are crews that regularly celebrate their heritage and collective identity through ritual, symbolism, folklore, and tradition. Whether it is worming or wagons, bugles on lapels or station tours, the firefighter is constantly being reminded that he is a part of something that is bigger than himself.

A tradition. A fellowship. A family. A community.

And because of these constant reminders, the firefighter remains anchored to a broader identity—one that gives purpose and meaning to the work.[26] A firefighter can walk into a fire station anywhere in the world, announce that he is a firefighter, and be instantly accepted into the family. Anywhere in the world!

Why?

Because firefighters share a collective identity, heritage, and tradition and regularly celebrate it as a community. They are a part of a very large and supportive family that is deeply anchored in tradition with rituals and artifacts that serve as constant reminders that they are a part of something larger than themselves.

Imagine if you could capture the same power in your organization. What would you stand to gain?

My simple advice to you:

Seek out and identify your corporate artifacts, symbols, folklore, and traditions, and create rituals to celebrate and honor them. Then watch what happens to your people, your services, and your organization.

SLEEPING WITH FAILURE

Everybody remembers where they were and what they were doing the morning of September 11, 2001, and I'm certainly no exception. I was at the fire marshal's office finishing up some final details for a presentation I was about to give to my employees. As the assistant fire marshal, I had been doing quite a bit of work with my staff to develop a new strategy for the fire marshal's office, which, because of explosive growth in the city, had been experiencing its highest workload in the department's 100-plus-year history.

The late 1990s and early 2000s saw the City of Austin as one of the fastest-growing cities in the nation, second only to Las Vegas. Austin was Boomtown, USA, and we were building homes, apartments, high rises, and commercial and industrial parks like they were going out of style. The city itself was flush with cash and was growing in size through annexations and in population through business and economic development, bringing to Austin the skilled labor and service industries that are ever-attendant to economic growth.

Lessons from the Line · 159

Austin is a funky and cool place to live and the University of Texas provides an ever-ready supply of keen minds to populate new and existing businesses. In the years before 9/11, every time you turned around some dot-com or high-tech firm was being founded, populated with young graduates, and subsequently taken public. Everybody was getting rich overnight. Twenty-four-year-olds became millionaires in the blink of an eye and then acted like you would expect a twenty-four-year-old millionaire to act. Spike-haired kids with pierced eyebrows were passing out business cards with titles such as "Executive Vice President of Everything" or "Chief of the Chief Operating Officers." Whatever dot-com, it didn't matter; it would succeed in Austin.

I like to refer to the late 1990s and early 2000s in Austin as the time of the Great Economic Illusion. People were fooled into thinking that wealth came with minimal effort and they were being set up for a colossal reality check. The ease with which wealth was created in those days was dizzying and difficult to believe. And while it may seem hackneyed to say, it warrants saying anyway—anything that appears too good to be true probably is. The Great Economic Illusion was nothing but a time bomb waiting for a fuse and ignition source, both of which the terrorists of September 11 were more than willing to provide.

While I was stacking the handouts for my presentation on the desk, one of my lieutenants popped his head into my office and said that a plane had hit the World Trade Center. "Again?" was my simple reply, remembering that New York had a history of such things.

"No, boss, this is different. We have the TV on. You'd better take a look."

Like so many people across the world, I stared in shocked silence as I watched the events of that dreadful day unfold. My entire staff joined me in front of the television in the "bullpen," the area where we establish the daily inspection agenda and where the lieutenants had their desks. Together, mesmerized by the unfolding drama, we stood and watched, helplessly, as thousands of innocent people vanished in an act of terrifying evil. Carl Wren, a very good friend and the fire department's chief fire protection engineer, upon seeing the first tower collapse, remarked to me, "Chief, there were a lot of firefighters in that building." All I could do was shake my head in disbelief.

After the second tower fell, I stood up and told my staff that I was going outside to get some fresh air. I did want some fresh air, but the truth is I was rapidly becoming concerned about my own city. Austin is the capital of Texas, which just so happens to be the home state of the president, who happens to be the former governor of Texas and a past oilman. Could Austin be a target, I wondered?

My office was situated right on the river downtown and it wasn't difficult to find a spot where I could see the state's Capitol building (which was rapidly being evacuated, I later learned). I found a seat and sat down and stayed there for an hour staring at the Capitol as a fearful spectator to the unfolding events of a world gone mad, wondering if the madness was about to visit my hometown. As I looked at the Capitol that morning, I found myself thinking what so many Americans probably thought that day, "How is this going to change my life, my career, my reality? What does all this mean?"

Gratefully, Austin was not a target of terrorism, and I slowly got up from my spectator's seat and went back to work, unaware that the events of that day had plugged a fuse into the Great Economic Illusion time bomb and unleashed a sequence of events that would quickly cause an explosion of a different character right in the middle of Austin, Texas. Neither my hometown nor my chosen profession would ever be the same again.

Economics is a difficult field of study and I don't claim to be an expert in the myriad and often confusing world of the invisible hand. But you don't have to be an expert in econometrics to understand that if a community's primary economic engines suffer a bust, everybody else in the area will bust with them. Prior to September 11, 2001, two of the primary industries that were driving the explosive growth in Austin were the high tech and the dot-coms. Two of the *hardest hit* industries by the post-9/11 economic correction were high tech and dot-com. Austin's economy was devastated almost overnight. It was a riches-to-rags story that took a dreadful toll on both the city itself and the people who worked in Austin and the surrounding areas. Layoffs were in the thousands, foreclosures were happening everywhere, unemployment skyrocketed, people experienced up to 50% decreases in their pay—but at least they had a job—and development came to a screeching standstill.

Perhaps the most compelling symbol of the Austin bust was the half-finished Intel building right in the middle of downtown. Like a skeleton of steel reaching skyward for a beautiful star that suddenly turned supernova, the Intel high-rise building was simply abandoned mid-project, leaving behind a shell that appeared half destroyed rather than half built. It was determined that the project was no longer economically viable for the company, so they simply walked away.

And then something terribly strange and disturbing started to happen in the city of Austin: people started to die in fires.

People die in fire. That's a fact. As long as humans continue to have access to sources of ignition, it's inevitable that we will have fires, and some of them will be deadly. The good news is that the fire service has learned a lot over the years about what causes and contributes to deadly fires, and we have incorporated our learning into the model codes that dictate how we build various structures, including homes, apartments, and high-rise buildings. It is largely due to these improvements in the design and construction of new structures that fire fatalities, on a national scale, are on the wane. What very few people understand, however, is that the model building and fire codes are progressive, meaning they are increasingly more prescriptive in their requirements for fire and life safety features as buildings and their uses increase in perceived risk.

For example, a high-rise building, due to the amount of people it can hold and its multiple and varied uses such as retail, commercial, office, entertainment, etc., represents a greater risk than does a two-story apartment complex. This risk is addressed by the codes through stringent requirements such as the provision of automatic sprinkler protection, pressurized stairwells, air movement and control devices, fire resistive construction, voice alarm systems, and more. Indeed, a modern high-rise structure built to today's standards is probably one of the safest buildings to be in during a fire. As the risk decreases, so do the requirements of the codes. This is why if you live in a single-family residence you are not required to have automatic sprinkler protection.[27]

The codes are designed to strike a balance between individual liberties and authority (prescribed safety). Think about that for a minute. We can protect you and your family from all fires by requiring you to live in concrete bunkers with no ignition sources in the constant presence of automatic sprinkler protection, but who would want to live there? If I told you that you would go to prison if I catch you drinking a bottle of vodka while smoking in bed, you would cry "foul!" and tell me that I was interfering with your personal liberties. And, of course, you would be right. Even though smoking in bed under the influence is a leading cause of fatal fires, I can't *force* you to stop. However, as you increase the number of people who can be exposed to the careless act of one person—say, your drinking and smoking in bed, for example—the codes increase in their requirements, limiting certain freedoms of few in the interest of many. This is why apartments have greater requirements than homes and high rises have greater requirements than apartments, and so on. Code officials, such as your fire marshal, are constantly walking a tightrope between these two sources of tension: personal liberties and safety. This tightrope can be terribly political and is, thus, a difficult rope to walk. Increases in safety always cost money, and those people who construct the buildings are trying to *make* money. You see the difficulty.[28]

Bottom line: the structures with the least fire and life safety code requirements and therefore the most individual liberties are private homes. It is precisely for this reason that most people die from fire in their homes. You can do whatever you want in your home and, generally speaking, it will only impact *you*.

The increase in fire fatalities didn't happen all at once in Austin. Like a slow drip from a leaking faucet that doesn't get your attention until the supporting wood rots out and suddenly the bottom falls out of the floor, it began slowly and kept up a steady pace throughout the year, gradually increasing momentum as one by one, people died in their homes from fire.

Meanwhile, my career took some turns. After 9/11 I requested a transfer back to combat operations and got it. I was reassigned as battalion chief supervising Battalion Two in northwest Austin. The events of 9/11 made me sick to my stomach and I wanted to do something, anything, to get back into the game; to reconnect, even if just in my own mind, to the brothers who died in those two towers. Even though it probably sounds silly to you, by requesting a combat assignment, I felt like I was engaging in the war on terror. September 11, 2001, changed all the rules, and overnight firefighters found themselves serving as frontline combatants in a global war. I wanted to be a part of it, even if my role was infinitesimally small. It's twisted but true—firefighters want to be near the danger. They want to be there when the Big One happens. If it was going to happen to Austin, I wanted to be a part of it.

But destiny had a different plan for me. Just four months into my new assignment I got a call from then Fire Chief Gary Warren. One of his assistant chiefs had retired and he invited me to apply for the job. Assistant fire chiefs, in most large fire departments, are appointed positions, meaning they are appointed at will by the current fire chief, as opposed to civil service promotion. Appointed positions give the fire chief the necessary flexibility to build a staff according to his or her specific needs in terms of talent, experience, background, and other factors. In May 2002, after a competitive process and an exhausting series of interviews, I was appointed to the rank of assistant fire chief and given the mantle of fire marshal for the City of Austin. It was with mild disappointment that I took the job as I realized I was out of the combat game forever.

I was wrong.

I have always been a data guy. I love numbers and believe they can tell a compelling story if we will just take the time to look at and evaluate them, whatever they may represent. I am convinced that many of the decisions we make in life—certainly in organizational life—we base not on data or solid information but rather on instinct, gut, experience, and intuition. These are certainly good tools to inform the decision-making process, but they aren't always reliable. So I took great pains over the years to develop meaningful metrics to assist my staff and me in making important decisions. Prior to my appointment to assistant fire chief, I had served as the city's assistant fire marshal for three years. In that time, with the assistance of a terrific staff, I had built a small data-crunching machine and regularly churned out meaningful statistics and data on how the fire department was performing. We would report our monthly metrics as a team and then post them on the board so that the entire staff could see how we were doing. It was fun and informative.

So, quite naturally, when I found myself back in the fire marshal's office, I requested a data summary of where we were and where we had been since my departure five months prior. What I saw shocked me.

The City of Austin averages about five fire fatalities a year, which is fairly standard for a city of its size. Consistent with national trends, the majority of these fatal fires occurred in the home. In May of 2002, however, we had already hit our annual average and we still had seven months to go. This was a disturbing trend given that we were now, apparently, averaging one death *per month*, and I said as much to my senior managers during our first weekly staff meeting after my appointment.

In my opinion, a good leader grows good leaders, surrounds himself with them, and then gets out of their way. As fire marshal, I had a stellar team of senior managers.

My assistant fire marshal was a battalion chief named Don Smith. A tall, lanky southern boy who reminded me of Ichabod Crane, Don was a veteran of the fire marshal's office. He had been there since he was a driver and he was hands down the most authoritative code expert in the department. Don and I had worked together for years and I had seen to it that he replaced me as assistant fire marshal when I left, in charge of the department's Inspections and Public Education divisions. My chief over the Fire/Arson Investigation Bureau was a guy named David Bailey. A fiercely intelligent man with a penchant for numbers like I had, Dave was the data go-to guy—the one who could crunch the numbers and see the nuances that made a difference. David was the famous "what-iffer" and I valued his intelligent company immensely. Finally, Carl Wren was my chief engineer. Carl is a soft-spoken, deeply religious man who is "every man's role model." Calm, brilliant (a rocket scientist by education), balanced, and wise, Carl kept all of us on course. If Don was the code ninja, Carl was the code scholar. He had written many of the model codes. Together, we made up the leadership team of the fire marshal's office for the City of Austin, and we took our jobs very seriously.

"According to this data, we're not exactly saving lives and property here, fellas," I said, as we looked over the new fatality data. "Is there anything we can learn from these fires?"

"Well, if you look at ignition scenarios, you can see an emerging trend," noted David. "Smoking appears to be the ignition source in most cases so far."

"But that's not exactly new information," corrected Carl. "Smoking is the leading cause of *all* fatal fires in America. Newsflash: we're just like the rest of the country."

Carl was right, of course. While most smokers don't realize it, that "tasty" cigarette is no different than a match, lighter, torch, or candle—an ignition source in search of a combustible, which it often finds. Indeed, cigarettes are seductively dangerous—from a fire-risk perspective—because they do not support an open flame and thus fool the user into thinking it is not dangerous. The truth is quite the opposite: a cigarette is designed to be a slow burner, which means it can support a form of slow combustion for several minutes, as opposed to seconds, as in the case of a match. Drop a cigarette into a foam couch or mattress and it will continue to burn unseen until it ignites the material, which can smolder for hours until it begins to burn freely. This is why so many smokers die hours after the cigarette has been carelessly dropped onto furniture, slowly setting the trap for their own killer fire.

"Have response times been an issue at any of these fires?" asked Don.

"I don't think so. In fact, the fires have all been pretty small. Little fires, lots of smoke, death by asphyxiation—the typical scenario," David said.

"Any red thread here, guys? Anything at all that links these fatal fires?" I asked.

"Other than the cigarettes, not that we can see so far, but we'll keep looking at it," David responded.

And so the conversation went for an hour or so as we looked at the data and explored various hypotheses on the apparent increase in fatal fires. Unfortunately, we couldn't find any emerging trend that was out of the ordinary, other than the obvious—that we were on course for a record year for fire deaths. David agreed to look into it more closely and even created a Fire Fatality Task Force to explore the issue in depth, and we agreed to meet on it again in the future.

Meanwhile, people kept dying. One by one, in the home, the bedroom, the living room, in apartments, in single-family residences, trapped in the bathroom while trying to get out, in vehicles—again and again, Austin residents were being killed by fire.

Not surprisingly, the trend quickly became a media story. "Another fire death in the City of Austin," the stories would go. "And yet again the Austin Fire Department reports one more death to the growing list of fire fatalities in our city." I remember specifically one reporter asking, "What's going on? Why are so many people dying from fire?"

Of course, we were asking the exact same question and weren't getting any answers. In time, my curiosity about the phenomena turned to obsession, and after we experienced our eleventh fire fatality—an African-American gentleman who had been a strong community leader in east Austin—my obsession turned to guilt. The media were out in force and the stories were deeply moving about the city's loss of a valued leader.

If this isn't our responsibility, whose is it? I remember thinking.

"We have got to figure out what is going on here, David!" I lamented over a cup of coffee one morning.

David and I were sitting in our favorite east Austin restaurant—Juan in a Million—sipping joe and eating one of Juan's famously delicious breakfast tacos. Juan had just stopped by our table to shake our hands and thank us like he did every time we were there, but today I didn't feel like we deserved it. I was on a full-scale rant and Dave was lending me an ear.

"David, if the city can't rely on its fire department to figure this stuff out, then why are we even here? Isn't it the department's job to see emerging trends, evaluate them, and then *do something* about it? I feel helpless!"

Scattered on the table in front of us were pictures from the multiple fatal fires, including the most recent. David and I had been looking them over and brainstorming possible causal scenarios, coming up empty handed, as usual.

"Well, the task force came up with a bunch of good ideas, Chief, but nothing that hasn't been tried before. Our firefighting efforts on these fires have been flawless; response times have been well within acceptable standards. The houses have been the full spectrum, modern to old, without any remarkable influence on the outcome. I just don't know."

As David was talking I was flipping through the pictures. I noticed one of the pictures was of a smoke alarm sitting beside the bed on a shelf, right next to where the victim had died.

"Which fire is this from?" I asked.

"The latest, I think. Why?"

"Check out the smoke detector. On a shelf next to the bed. Lotta good that did him," I whined.

"Didn't do him any good. It had no battery and it wasn't even mounted. We see that a lot nowadays," David said casually.

"Really? How often?" I asked, leaning forward to see the picture better.

"Well, now that you mention it, Chief, all the time. I can't say for sure, but I'll bet each fire where somebody died in their home, they did so in the absence of a working smoke alarm," David said matter-of-factly.

I stared at David for a long minute and it was obvious that we were both thinking the same thing. I finally said, "Find out for sure." It was not a request.

And that's how it started. David and his staff went back and re-examined the files for every single fatal fire that had occurred in a home or structure and, sure enough, in every single case the person had died in a home that had a nonworking smoke alarm. The smoke alarm was there, mind you. It was not working either because it was old or the battery had been removed. *Every—single—case.* A fifteen-dollar piece of plastic with a working battery could have saved a life.

"Can that be it? Surely it can't be that simple." I asked during a staff meeting later in the year.

"Maybe," said Carl. "It is compelling, and we certainly have an emerging public education message that we need to get out. But, is it just a coincidence? Good question. Here's what we do know: a smoke alarm increases your chances of surviving a fire by 50% or more. It isn't fail-safe, but it is an effective tool against fire. Most of our fatal fires were small and the cause of death was asphyxiation, so it logically follows that a working smoke alarm would have alerted them to the fire and given them time to get out. This could be our problem, Chief. If this is not *the* problem, then it certainly is *a* problem," Carl said, always the rational one.

The truth is I was skeptical. Like crime or health care, there are so many variables that can influence a fatal outcome of a fire that it just didn't seem practical or even reasonable to think that a fifteen-dollar piece of plastic was responsible for what appeared to be the city's worse year ever for fatal fires. Everybody knows to check their smoke alarm anyway, I reasoned; that has been our central safety message for more than twenty years now. Change your batteries twice a year. "Spring forward, fall back," everybody knows this. We teach smoke-alarm awareness everywhere we go, in schools, churches, places of business, our marketing material, everywhere. Having a working smoke alarm is not a new message in the City of Austin; we've been harping about it for years.

My staff and I talked about it some more and agreed that we needed to explore the efficacy of our existing literature on smoke alarms and let it go at that. In hindsight, I think that was the most dreadfully shortsighted decision of my entire fire service career. To this day I still have a hard time sleeping with that decision, and it occasionally keeps me up late into the night staring wide-eyed at the ceiling.

Why? Because on Christmas Eve of 2002, in the span of one hour, four people would die from fire in the City of Austin; three of them would be little boys. The house where the boys died had three smoke alarms, and best we

Lessons from the Line · 173

can tell not a single one of them worked. The other death was in a small bungalow downtown: a smoke alarm without a battery.

When I got the call from dispatch early in the morning that Christmas Eve, I almost threw up. My stomach was heaving as I sat on the edge of the bed with my face in my hands; I moaned while my wife stroked my neck and told me it wasn't my fault.

"I don't think it's an issue of fault, honey," I finally said. "I know it's not my fault. It is, however, an issue of responsibility." And with that I got up, put on my uniform, and headed to the fire scene. David was there waiting on me, his investigators in tow.

It was freezing that morning as I toured the scene under David's guidance. He told me that the boys' father had made a valiant effort to rescue the boys, even going so far as to set a ladder to the upstairs window, breaking it out, and attempting to enter the burning house. He was seriously injured in the process. David also informed me that the firefighters had been incredibly heroic as well, entering the upstairs area without hand line protection in an attempt to get to the boys and going as far as they could without dying in the effort themselves. "They did a good job, Chief. They just couldn't get to them in time."

"Talk to me about the smoke alarms, David. Are you sure they weren't working?" I asked as we watched the Medical Examiner load up the boys.

"Chief, we can find no indication that they worked and we're absolutely sure that two of the three weren't operational. None of the responding firefighters heard a smoke alarm. We can't find any bystanders that heard one. We've looked the detectors over thoroughly and they do not appear to be functional. And then there is the obvious—they didn't get out alive."

"Can I say with confidence that there were no working smoke alarms?" I asked.

"Chief, you get the big bucks for a reason. You decide. But I am confident, and so are my people, that they weren't working."

"Okay," I said with a sigh as I turned to face the media horde that had assembled on the other side of our barrier tape.

Put yourself in my shoes for a moment, dear reader. You think you know what the problem is, but there are three boys over there who just died, another death downtown, and lots of grieving mothers, fathers, friends, and relatives who probably aren't interested in hearing you talk about *their* nonworking smoke alarms. You are surrounded by dozens of reporters: print, radio, local affiliates, wire service, journalists from all over the state; you know your words will make national news. Cameras are everywhere, but mostly in your face. You can use this as an opportunity to give them what they want to hear—the grim story—or use it as a chance to give them what they *need* to hear. What will you do?

As I stood before the media that day, I suddenly felt tired. Not just a little tired, but flat-out exhausted. Spent. All I

Lessons from the Line · 175

wanted to do was go home, drink a beer, and go to bed. I looked at the reporters with weary eyes and finally stood up straight and told myself to get off the pity pot and get to work.

As I took a deep breath to start my interview, I remembered my grandfather's advice: *Kevin, dare to do what you think is right, not what you think is safe.*

I swallowed hard, and this is what I said:

"Get up from wherever you are, whatever you're doing, Right Now! And test your smoke detector!" I yelled it, sending the reports reeling. "If it's not working, change the battery. If you still can't get it to work, go buy a new one! If you can't find a store that's open, call the fire department and we'll come out and put one in for you! *Just … do … it … right … now!*" I screamed, reaching a crescendo as I finished.

The reporters stared at me, stunned by my passion, microphones hung in mid-air, suspended in time. I'm sure my passion and earnestness looked a whole lot like anger to them, and in fact one reporter told me after the fact that she thought I was about to bite her head off. I didn't mean it that way. I was just sick of what seemed to me to be senseless and certainly preventable death—on *my* watch, no less. It was a classic "This is my failure so I'm going to scream at you" approach. But it had its desired effect. The journalists quickly recovered from my unexpected outburst and we spent the next twenty minutes talking about smoke alarms and their life-saving virtues.

And, finally, after nineteen fire fatalities in twelve months and a terribly emotional Christmas Eve, the City of Austin slowly began to wake up to its emerging fire safety problem.

The public reaction to the press conference on the scene that terrible morning was overwhelming. We received more than a hundred calls from concerned citizens asking us what they could do to help—volunteer, send money, donate detectors, and more. All of the local television affiliates offered their services to shoot public safety announcements and run them during primetime, which we did immediately. The *Austin American Statesman* ran a series of front-page stories about smoke alarms and the Austin fire fatality problem. For several days after the fire, stories ran in the press about the terrible tragedy and whether smoke alarms would have made a difference. The message made it all the way to the national news: "Three die in Christmas fire. Get a working smoke detector!"

The week after the fire, back in my office, I got a call from a woman named Janice Godwin. She introduced herself as the president of Special Audience Marketing, a local advertising firm.

"We saw your press conference last week and it blew us away. Clearly we have a local problem that requires a local message. Can we help you?" Janice said earnestly.

"We would love some help, Janice," I replied. "And we certainly need some help because obviously our efforts to get the word out have been ineffectual. But I have very limited resources for this, so my hands are somewhat tied."

"Not a problem, Kevin. This is a pro bono offer. When do you want to begin work?" she said.

Surprised by her generosity, I said the only word that came to mind, "Now." And we set up an appointment for later in the week.

By this time I was feeling pretty good about my decision that morning at the fire. It was a risk, but it appeared to be paying off, I thought. The word was getting out and we were creating some momentum for change. Major changes in behavior and policy always occur on the heels of tragedy. It's a drag, but it's a fact. *I have a responsibility to the citizens of Austin and it's my job to communicate the truth, even if it hurts,* I reasoned. Maybe by the death of the three boys, other lives can be saved. Of what value were their deaths if we do not learn from them? Such was my thinking. That is, until I received a letter from the boys' family.

It came by e-mail and it was addressed specifically to me. The letter was from the boys' uncle,[29] the brother of the man who was injured trying to save their lives that morning. He was writing on behalf of his brother, and he was angry. It isn't necessary to share the specific language of the letter; I can summarize very simply for you what it said: "Chief Baum, please stop what you are doing. *It's killing us.*"

I read the letter several times, staring wide-eyed at my computer before I got up and walked to the door of my office. I closed and locked the door and went back to my desk and sat in my chair, stunned by what I had just read. Finally, I turned the chair so that I could look out the window and see Town Lake. It was a beautiful winter day in Austin—clear skies reflecting off the glass-like water with kayaks snaking their lazy way along the stream, little rivulets of wakes trailing behind them. *An Ansel Adams picture*, I thought, *beautiful.*

And then I started crying. Deep sobs from the well of my soul. Like waves, the emotions washed over me again and again, and I just let it happen. As I sat there that day looking at the river through tears, I was thinking one simple thought: *My God, what have I done?*

It took me several days to process that letter and to muster the courage to write back to the family. I knew that I owed them an explanation and deep within me, in an area I didn't want to explore, I knew that I personally had caused them great pain by my actions. It didn't come as a surprise to me to learn that they were hurting, and I was smart enough to know that my media blitz could only add to their pain. But I reasoned that I had no choice. It was my responsibility to *do something*. So I simply forced myself to think forward, not back; and in that way I could insulate myself from the pain I was causing; pretend it wasn't there. Indeed, it's easy to rationalize a leadership decision when everybody is patting you on the back. But look real consequence right in the face and let's see what happens to your leadership resolve.

That letter was a real consequence—right in my face—and marked a turning point in my career and my life. I struggled with that letter and what it represented for several days, and even more sleepless nights.

Three things resulted from my struggle. The first was a reaffirmation that the career choice I made involved death. The fire service mission is to save lives and property, but history has taught us that we will never be fully successful in this purpose. "Failure" in the fire service is a constant; what should define us is how we deal with this failure when we encounter it, not the fact that it happened on our watch. But face it we must.

The second result of my struggle was a simple realization: leadership is always uncomfortable. Period. Leadership always involves risk, and risk is always uncomfortable. Everybody wants to be a leader on a sunny day, but as all firefighters know, every day isn't sunny.

And finally, I made a decision: embrace the discomfort, Kevin, or get out of the game. Leaders should expect to have sleepless nights. If they don't, it's likely they aren't leading. *In or out,* I thought. *Make a decision and make it now.*

I decided to stay in.

In fact, I decided that I would make it my personal mission to stay the course and finish what I had started—to see something good come out of the terrible tragedies of 2002. So I wrote back to the family and expressed my deepest sympathies and apologized for causing them further pain. But I also explained why it was so important, even urgent, to learn from our fire experience and incorporate that learning into our actions in order to save future lives with what we have learned. And, in fact, isn't that what you want your fire department to do for you? It was a difficult letter to write and even more difficult to send. But it was an important conversation to have.

And we kept moving forward.

It took us six months to create a new fire safety message for our city. Special Audience Marketing, by the time it was all said and done, had contributed more than $50,000 of time and resources for free to help us create an educational campaign. We approached the project scientifically, conducting focus groups of volunteers and asking them a variety of prepared questions on fire safety and smoke-alarm awareness. We then tabulated the results and looked for the common themes that might help to build an effective message. Interestingly, of all the data to come out of those focus groups, the only common theme was that, at the very least, everybody knows *how* to test a smoke alarm. You push the little red button with your finger.

So the ad agency ran with the finger theme and created Freddy Finger—a smoke alarm sticking his finger in the air to test the alarm, with the slogan, "Give Fire the Finger!"

We wanted a crunchy message that would get people's attention, and Freddy's message, "Give Fire the Finger," was pretty darn crunchy. Madonna once said, "There's no such thing as 'bad' press." We knew that the double-meaning of the message would cause a stir; in fact, we wanted it to. We figured that a public stir, even if a bit scandalous, could only help to get the word out about smoke alarms, and we wanted to get the word out. Serious circumstances warrant serious risk, we reasoned. I loved the message. The fire chief loved it. Everybody loved it except the city manager, who thought it presented too much of a risk. So, we went back to the drawing board and softened Freddy's message to "Put a Finger on It!" obviously telling you to test your smoke alarm. Not as crunchy, but still effective. The new message was almost ready to launch.

Initial mockup of the Freddy Finger campaign. The message was later revised. Reprinted with permission from Special Audience Marketing, Austin, Texas.

Final mockup of the Freddy Finger campaign. This version of Freddy Finger is today saving lives across the nation and the world. Reprinted with permission from Special Audience Marketing, Austin, Texas.

Meanwhile, people kept dying from fire in Austin and in every single case they did so in the absence of a working smoke alarm. We were in a race with the Grim Reaper. And we were losing big time.

We introduced Freddy to the world in late July 2003.

If you've ever been to Austin in the summer months before it gets too hot, you have probably had the opportunity to enjoy the Zilker outdoor theater. The Zilker Theatre Production is a non-profit group with a fifty-year history of providing wonderful entertainment to Austin families and visitors, all in an outdoor venue located right in the middle of downtown. Classic Austin, the outdoor theater attracts thousands of people of all ages to a full-length Broadway musical accompanied by snow cones, popcorn, and laughter. It's a great time and was a perfect place to introduce Freddy to the world. Graciously, the theater group offered to partner with the department by letting us use the venue to tell our story.

I took the stage in late July 2003 and told the people in the audience about Austin's terrible track record for fire deaths. I walked them through the ugly events of 2002, culminating in the Christmas Eve tragedy. I was as graphic as I dared to be, hoping to knock them off balance and get their attention. Even though it was an outdoor venue, you could've heard a pin drop as I finished my grim soliloquy that night. I had their attention. Finally, as a group of firefighters unfurled a banner of Freddy with his message, I told the audience that there was hope. A simple piece of plastic, a fifteen-dollar investment, is all you need to get out alive.

"What value do you put on your own life and that of

your kids?" I asked. "More than fifteen dollars? What about a three-dollar battery? Is your husband's life worth that much?" I probed. "Go home tonight and test your smoke alarms. Before you do anything else, put a finger on that red button and make sure it works. Put a finger on it!"

I screamed it, and then made the audience shout the message over and over, each person holding his or her finger up in the Freddy gesture. It was fantastic and the audience really got into the energy of the event, media cameras rolling. I had chills on my neck as their voices boomed that night, ricocheting off the hills and echoing off the river's stillness, sending a loud and clear message to our city that the time had come to fight back.

The next day, every single Austin fire crew hit the streets (forty stations). We had equipped each station with hundreds of Freddy Finger door hangers. On one side of the flyer was Freddy and his "Put A Finger on It!" message. On the flip side was text outlining four simple things you can do to make sure your smoke alarm will work for you when you need it. The crews spent an entire afternoon canvassing their response territories and hanging these flyers on the doors of homes, apartments, and businesses. The media rode out with the crews and told the story that night.

"Austin firefighters are fighting back and need your help," the reporters said. "Look to your door to find out how!" It was a great way for our crews to mingle with the community they serve while sharing important life safety information. Freddy had hit the streets and I was starting to take heart that we were going to turn things around.

We introduced Freddy on a Saturday night and spent Sunday spreading the word. On Monday, a beautiful young lady died from fire, bringing the City of Austin's eighteen-month fire death total to a staggering twenty-four.[30] The young lady came home tired, smoked in bed, and fell asleep. She later died of asphyxiation from a smoldering mattress, ignited by her cigarette. On her front door, hanging uselessly, was Freddy Finger and his message, and just inside the door on a coffee table was a smoke alarm. It had been disassembled.[31] Once again I found myself on the scene of a fatal fire, surrounded by reporters and cameras.

As tragic as that young woman's death was, it served as the tipping point for the City of Austin and smoke alarm awareness. People watched in horror that night as the reporters showed pictures of Freddy hanging on the young lady's door—twisted irony in a terrible fight against fire. The poor woman had to have walked right past Freddy and his message as she went into her home that night. The stories were compelling and an entire community started to get up and test its smoke alarms.

From the day that young lady died, the City of Austin went eighteen months without a single fire death. *Not one.* In the eighteen months prior to her death, from the time we realized we had a problem to the time we released the Freddy Finger campaign, twenty-four Austinites would be dead from fire. In the eighteen months following, that number would drop to zero.[32] Yes, zero. The city would experience only one fire fatality in twenty-four months after Freddy's introduction, and a working smoke alarm wouldn't have made a difference.[33] What's even more compelling is the score of citizens that called the department and gave testimony to Freddy's effectiveness. They usually called in tears to tell us that they had a fire and got out alive because they had replaced their smoke alarms after hearing our Freddy Finger story.

Freddy Finger door hanger, hanging uselessly on the door of the city's final fire fatality in 2003. The occupant walked right past Freddy and his message and died later that night from fire. Her smoke alarm was disassembled on a table in the living room. Picture by Bob Parker, taken from the Kevin Baum library.

Smoke alarms, like any other piece of technology, fail over time. They age, get dirty, dusty, removed, and so forth. It is inevitable, given enough time, that your smoke alarm will fail. Unfortunately, without testing, you will only discover this when you need it the most. Like any other piece of technology, your smoke alarm needs constant care, maintenance, testing, and cleaning. To not take care of your smoke alarm(s) is as foolish as driving a car with bald tires with your kids in the back seat not wearing seat belts. You wouldn't do that, would you? Get up right now and test your smoke alarm. Your life may depend upon it.

It was just before Christmas 2004, and I was at home tinkering around the house when the phone rang. As soon as the caller introduced herself I knew I was in for a difficult conversation. The caller was Sarah Lagrone. Sarah was the mother of one of the boys that died in the Christmas Eve fire of 2002. Our conversation was awkward and bumpy at first, neither of us knowing exactly what to say to the other. Finally, Sarah found her voice and told me why she was calling.

"Kevin, after the fire I was angry. I was angry at the world, at the department, and, frankly, angry with you in particular. All the noise about smoke alarms just made me sick, and I wanted to crawl away and hide." As she spoke, I could feel that old familiar guilt clawing its way back into my soul.

"But over time my anger turned to grief, and then it

just became a dull ache. I finally started to mourn, and now, after two years, I think I'm ready to get involved so that this doesn't happen to any other mothers and so they don't have to go through what I went through. I've been watching everything that has happened since I lost my son, all the smoke alarm stuff and the success you've had, and I was wondering, can I get involved? Can I help?"

As I listened I got tears in my eyes and I knew on the other end of that line was one of the most courageous individuals I had ever met. Sarah got involved and is still involved to this day. In fact, Freddy is now saving lives across the world. See for yourself at www.firepreventioncampaigns.org.

LESSON FROM THE LINE
ORGANIZATIONAL LEARNING

"You don't drown by falling in the water, you drown by staying there."

Edwin Louis Cole

"Men succeed when they realize that their failures are the preparation for their victories."

Ralph Waldo Emerson

"Failure should be our teacher, not our undertaker."

Dr. Denis Waitley

A couple of years ago I was hired by one of America's largest counties to provide a series of workshops on performance diagnostics—in-depth training on how to thoughtfully explore data and make meaningful decisions based on what the data is telling us. It was an exciting opportunity for me as I had just retired from the fire department and was building my consulting practice from a part-time venture to a full-time career. It was also an exciting opportunity for the county as it planned to train every senior manager and executive in the organization—1,200 in all. I had convinced the county's general managers that real organizational change could only occur if they "trained to the tipping point" by engaging enough managers and leaders to create an enterprise-wide buzz for positive cultural change. They agreed, and I began an exhausting but incredibly rewarding five-month marathon of workshops.

A central theme in my diagnostics program is the power of failure as a tool for organizational learning. With the Freddy Finger story as the centerpiece, through a series of case studies I explored the value of failure and demonstrated that it is not the failure itself that defines a person or an organization. Rather, it is how we respond to that failure that is the defining quality. I informed the managers that great people and organizations are not defined by their times, as the history books would tell us, but are defined by *how they react* to the times where they find themselves. World War II didn't define Churchill, Churchill defined Churchill; the Civil War didn't define Lincoln, Lincoln defined Lincoln. It is our reaction to what happens around us that defines us, not the event itself.

I told the managers that they should, therefore, face their failures, rather than fear them—name it, claim it, and explain it. Name it: this is failure. Claim it: this occurred on my watch, therefore I own it. Explain it: tell the world what you intend to do about it. Failure is inherently human, I explained. To deny or fear failure is to fear life itself.

I continued the discussion by demonstrating that the fear of failure results in risk-averse behavior, risk-averse behavior leads to complacency, and complacency ultimately yields mediocrity. "Are you content with mediocrity?" I would ask. Facing failure head on is a powerful tool for learning and growth, so stop worrying about perceptions and start thinking about performance.

This particular county employs some of the most thoughtful, educated, and professional managers I have ever encountered. Many of the managers are downright brilliant, stellar government leaders who truly care about public service and their role as public servants. And yet, after every single workshop, at least a half dozen of these managers would come up to me and say, "Your message about failure is compelling and right on the mark. But you should know, Kevin, this is not a failure-friendly culture. Failure is not accepted around here."

"So what do you do with failure when you see it?" I would ask.

"Hide it. Keep it secret. Limit the risks we take," was often the reply.

As if to confirm that the fear of failure was a cultural norm in this organization, after a series of silly communication errors, I confused my itinerary and scheduled a flight for the wrong day to make a series of workshops. I realized the error a day before I was supposed to be there, and I immediately called my county contact, a senior manager in the HR department, to inform him of the mistake.

The workshops had become extremely popular and all the programs for that week had been booked months in advance. It would be very difficult for the busy managers to rearrange their calendars.

"I don't know how we got it wrong and I've tried to book another flight, but it looks like I'm going to miss the first day," I told him.

"What are we going to do?" he asked.

"Send an e-mail apology and tell them that it was a communication error, and let's pick a day to reschedule the workshops."

"No. We can't tell them this was our mistake. Some of our most senior people are supposed to be there. How about this—I'll tell them there were problems with the airlines and it was the airline's fault you can't get out here. What do you think?" he said.

I stared at my telephone, frankly wondering if he was serious, and finally replied, "I think that wouldn't be the truth. I have a better idea: let's just tell them what really happened—you can blame it on me, if you want to—and let the chips fall where they may. There isn't a single person scheduled for those workshops that's perfect, so I'm pretty sure they don't expect perfection from us. I do know that they expect us to be honest, though."

"I really think that's a bad idea, Kevin." He was genuinely concerned about this.

"This was an honest mistake," I reassured him. "Let's not make a dishonest one in an attempt to cover it up."

We sent the e-mail and rescheduled the training for another day. Other than that, nothing happened. The managers were experienced enough to realize that errors occur. It may have been an inconvenience, but that was all, and we fixed the mistake. However, my contact with the county was genuinely afraid of serious consequences and his fear of admitting a slight failure was very real.

After I completed my workshop series, I was asked to present at a county executive's quarterly meeting. All of the county's top executives would be in attendance, and they were eager to hear how the training had gone and what I had heard from the workforce. The county executive officer and his general managers were all there as well. As I stood up to visit with the executives, I decided to walk my talk and take a risk.

"I am convinced that you are one of the best-managed, if not *the* best-managed county in America," I started, and I meant it. Lots of smiles and nodding heads.

"Your managers are stellar and your capacity for accomplishment is off the charts. However, there is one thing holding you back from real greatness, from truly setting your county apart from the crowd, and I have heard it from all of your managers." I had their attention now, so I paused for effect and then told them the truth.

"There is a culture of fear in your organization. There is a very real fear of failure in this county and it is manifested by a hesitancy to take risks and a fear to step out of acceptable comfort zones. There are two problems with this culture of fear," I warned. "The first is the obvious. If your managers fear failure and its consequences, when they do fail—and they will because we all do—they are going to hide it. Failure doesn't get better with age, it just gets worse. In fact, its additive in its effect. Little failure here, little failure there, in time these hidden failures will combine to create one colossal failure, and that could be catastrophic. Remember, if we are not willing to name failure when we see it, it's likely we are rewarding it. What could be the consequences of that?"

It was a rhetorical question, but I had their attention and they were all staring at me, wondering where this conversation would lead.

"The second problem is that this culture of fear serves as a disincentive to your managers to taking risks and from trying unconventional approaches to improve performance. If we aren't innovating, taking risks, and exposing ourselves to the possibility of failure, then we aren't trying anything new. If we aren't trying anything new, then we aren't learning and growing as an organization. And if we aren't learning and growing then, folks, what's the point?"

"Bottom line: a fear of failure does exist in this organization. I've met with twelve hundred of your managers—many sitting in this room right now—and they all say the same thing, 'Failure is not okay in this county.' So, here's my question to all of you, the leadership of this county: Where does a fear of failure get its start? Where does it originate?"

The silence that followed was terribly unsettling, and I began to wonder if I had stepped out too far and breached the consultant-client relationship through a semi-public admonishment. And then the county executive officer himself came up to the podium and took the microphone. He spoke loud and clear.

"If there is a culture of fear in this organization, then I accept full responsibility. It's my fault." You could almost hear a gasp throughout the room, a rippling wave as managers and executives shifted in their seats.

"You all know that I do not like surprises, and that won't change. But I never said that I don't want our people to take risks, to try new things, to fail if necessary to improve performance. I welcome innovation. We need innovation. So, if there is a culture of fear in this county, I want you all to know that I take the blame. However, I do not accept all the responsibility for turning this around. Everyone sitting in this room shares the responsibility with me to encourage our people to get out of their comfort zones, to take risks, to change this culture of fear. We share that responsibility, and I expect you to hold me to it, as I will you."

It was an incredible demonstration of leadership.

One year later the National Association of Counties gave this chief executive officer and his county more awards for outstanding performance in public service than any county has ever received in the history of the awards program. It is indeed the best-managed county in America.

I share this story as a prelude to this lesson because it highlights what I believe to be an all-too-common pathology in organizational life today; obviously I'm talking about the fear of failure. If I have learned anything from all my travels over the years working with organizations, and if my own experiences in the fire service have taught me anything (particularly the terrible fire fatality experience), it is that a fear to recognize and claim failure when we see it only *leads to more failure.* Think about that for a minute. If we constantly have our heads in a foxhole, hiding from risk and failure, how do we ever expect to get out? It is impossible to have your eyes on the horizon when your head is in a foxhole or to think creatively or strategically when you're constantly running for cover!

Winston Churchill once said, "If you are going through hell, keep going." Churchill was obviously telling us that when we find ourselves in a bad situation, the only way out is to keep moving; standing still does nothing. What I see all too often in organizations today, however, is that when we find ourselves in hell (serious failure), we generally dig a "foxhole" and tell ourselves and our peers, "This too shall pass." Or, worse yet, we hide in our foxholes and occasionally jump up to throw volleys of blame at somebody else.[34] Either way, you're still in hell.

I am fascinated with the general fear of failure that appears to exist in organizations today, and I am convinced it is one of the single greatest impediments to organizational improvement. Indeed, I think this is so important I have spent the past several years interviewing my clients and audiences in an effort to discover what is going on.

Not surprisingly, when I ask them why we fear failure, I get a variety of answers, including the perception of incompetence, the fear of consequence, embarrassment, and so forth. People just don't like to fail, but in a very real sense they can't tell you why, and I've asked thousands of them over the years. What's more, if you ask them whether or not they have ever failed, they always answer "yes." Every one of them. So here's the urgent question: If failure is such a common experience of the human condition, why do we fear it so much? Particularly, why do we fear it in organizational life?

After years of exploring this question with my clients and peers and reflecting on this question in light of my own personal failures, here is what I think is going on in organizations today and, as leaders, what I want you to consider: *People incorrectly associate failing with losing.*

People think that to fail is to lose, and nobody wants to be a loser. The fear of being considered a loser, especially in organizational life, is a powerful motivator to any of a host of deviant behaviors, including hiding failure, cooking up numbers to tell a different story, blaming our performance shortfalls on somebody else or some other group, or flat out denying that it even happened. And when these behaviors become the norm, they plant seeds of distrust and resentment, fomenting a destructive culture that will fester within an organization and lead to further failure and deceit. It becomes a vicious and destructive pattern.

But here's the irony and also the good news: failing and losing are different things! Failing is a fact of life. We are all human and to be human is to be imperfect. We will all fail from time to time. What separates the winners from the losers is not the failure itself, but *what we do with the failure.* Failure in the pursuit of an objective is still success if we learn and grow from the experience. But what's terribly ironic and disturbing is that the powerful fear of being considered a loser actually causes many people to *act like one!*

We only lose in organizational life when we fail to take action on failure when we see it. That's when we become losers and that's when, in my opinion, individuals should suffer consequences.

Leaders today have got to make room for failure. They've got to let their people know that acknowledging failure when you see it is not a bad thing but a good thing, so long as you can demonstrate that you are trying to do something about it. Indeed, I am convinced that there is great nobility in naming failure when you see it and then demonstrating that you have a plan of action to address the problem, or at least that you are considering options and could use some help. Nobody expects you to be perfect, but they do expect you to be honest, to learn, and to not repeat the same mistakes.

Watching people die from fire at an unprecedented rate is a good definition of hell, especially if you are tasked with preventing that very thing from happening. The City of Austin's experience in fire deaths was, in my opinion, failure on a grand scale, and I considered that failure to be mine. It would have been incredibly easy to claim that the department had no control over the deaths. After all, we can't control what humans do in their homes, and hey, people *do die* in fires. It would have been just as easy to look at historical records and make the claim that the increase in fire fatalities was just a statistical spike. Public safety tragedies, like hurricanes, come and go and some years are worse than others. Hunker down and "This too shall pass."

By hiding from failure when you see it, you're really just taking the easy road by shifting the blame and the responsibility—an avoidance behavior to prevent the real and disturbing work of looking the failure right in the face and asking some difficult questions. If you do take the easy road, consider carefully the consequences of your inaction. Are you comfortable with dooming your organization to repeating failures, over and over again until somebody else steps up and cries "Stop!"?

Which is easier to sleep with at night: facing, naming, and claiming failure when you see it with all the attendant risks and unknowns, or fearing it and running from it, ensuring that it will repeat itself at a later date?

You decide.

THE DRAGON SLAYER IN YOU

I have a strange relationship with Mt. Rainier—a relationship that, try as I may, I can't seem to explain in a way that people will understand. A beautiful 14,411-foot glaciated volcano in the Pacific Northwest, just a three-hour drive from Seattle, Mt. Rainier represents a little bit of Alaska right here in the lower forty-eight states and has played a key role in my life over the past several years. In fact, in ten attempts to climb that mountain over the past ten years, I've only been to the top twice. But I keep going back. The mountain draws me.

George Mallory, a British climber who died trying to become the first person to stand on the summit of Mt. Everest, is famous for his reply to a *New York Times* journalist who wanted to know why he was interested in climbing such an unforgivable mountain. In reply, Mallory simply said, "Because it is there."[35] I don't think Mallory was trying to be evasive or cheeky with his response. Rather, I think his reply represents an acceptance on his part that it is impossible to adequately communicate why somebody wants to climb a mountain or do anything extremely risky for that matter. So, rather than trying to explain something that is intensely personal, he simply said the obvious, "Because it is there." His quote today is famous and is used in a wide variety of contexts to explain that which people find to be unexplainable.

Regardless, when I use it, people generally seem less than satisfied with the explanation.

My infatuation with climbing in general and Mt. Rainier in particular began in June of 1996. At the time, I was assigned to Ladder Thirty-two as captain and station officer. This was a dual assignment as Station Thirty-two, in addition to housing a ladder and engine company, also housed the department's Technical Rescue Team. The ten firefighters that were assigned to Station Thirty-two on each shift were cross-trained in special rescue techniques, including cave rescue, high-rise rescue, confined space rescue, swift water rescue, and more. It was an exciting assignment for me, and while the training commitment was constant, I didn't mind because I was learning all kinds of new skills, particularly skills in rope craft.

If there is any constant at all in special rescues, it's the need for ropes, knots, and anchors. Whatever predicament somebody is capable of getting him or herself into, with a rope, some carabineers, and anchors, I bet your fire department can get that person out. So, not surprisingly, we would spend hours each shift at Station Thirty-two tying knots, competing with each other to see who could rig the fastest anchors or mechanical advantage systems,[36] rappelling and ascending ropes, and goofing off in the "Spider Web."

Tommy Gillis, the lieutenant in charge of Engine Thirty-two and hands down the most resourceful man I have ever known, spent hours rigging a complicated network of ropes and anchors along the ceiling of the truck-room bays. Station Thirty-two maintains a three-bay garage, so there was a lot of space to create a tangled web of ropes along the ceiling. By the time he was done rigging it, the ceiling was a menagerie of crisscrossed ropes, rappel lines (to quickly escape the web in the event we got a call), and anchors. To top it off, several of the firefighters assigned to Station Thirty-two made a massive black spider out of paper and cardboard and stuck it high in the tangled web of ropes. Christened "Charlotte's Web," the network of ropes was created to serve as a training system, but it was much more entertainment than work. We would spend hours ascending the ropes, traversing lines using prussic and Jumar systems, swinging like Tarzan from rappel line to rappel line, transferring lines, bypassing knots, and just hanging from the ceiling hooting and hollering at each other. The number of goofy games we came up with to compete with each other on that "training" web was hilarious. But it was still just training, and in a controlled environment no less; so, once a month or so, we would take our skills into the field and give them a real test.

Austin is the gateway to the Edwards Plateau, an elevated region of land created long ago during the Cretaceous Period, and a stunning piece of landscape. Locals simply call the area "the hill country." Drive thirty minutes west of Austin during a sunny spring day and you will feel as if you were just transported to the foothills of the Blue Mountains. Round rolling hills with dense canopies of oak, cedar, and elm, the area is spectacularly beautiful. Adding to its natural appeal is the Highland Lakes System, a series of dams and reservoirs that channel and store the Colorado River; this waterway cuts right through the hill country creating breathtaking cliffs and powerfully romantic sunset vistas. The hill country adds immeasurably to the Austin quality of life, as it offers ample waterways, cliffs, and caves in which the outdoor enthusiasts can play and firefighters can train.

We would spend entire days training in the hills, building anchors, practicing lost-man searches, and conducting mock rescues. We would package a "patient," usually the rookie, into a rescue stretcher and give him the ride of his life, transporting him over swift water on a high-line system, lowering him into and out of caves, and dropping him off the side of 100-foot high-rise buildings. It was a time of great personal challenge—a daily face-your-fear confrontation and confidence builder. And after every training event, I would feel stronger and more capable. In time, I began to characterize these training challenges as "feeding the dragon slayer within," a double entendre to the universal label of firefighting: Dragon Slaying.

I specifically remember one caving experience that pushed me to the limit. Caving was *never* my strong suit. In fact, I used to tell my firefighters that caves were created for rats, moles, and cockroaches, so why would a human even go into one? It just seems unnatural to me. But the reality is that a lot of people enjoy caving and sometimes they get into trouble. So we did quite a bit of training in caves, and every time we went underground it was a major challenge for me. It wasn't the physical act of slithering around holes that bothered me so much as my horrific fear of tight places. Even though it was unspoken, Tommy sensed my fear of the underworld and would always keep a cautious eye on me when we were in caves. As the officers of the team, Tommy and I both believed that we shouldn't ask our people to do anything that we ourselves weren't capable of doing. This policy normally wasn't a problem and as long as we were jumping off buildings and cliffs, I was okay. But underground I rapidly became mush.

We were on a training mission and were deep underground in a cave in south Austin. As usual, I was pulling up the rear when we came to a hole that I just couldn't go in. It was roughly the size of a human torso and twice as long and made a gradual ninety-degree turn upward as you went through it. To get through, you had to take off your helmet and gear, get on your back, and slither through using your hands and feet for propulsion, all the while pushing your gear ahead of you while the top of the hole scratched your nose raw. You had to do this in complete darkness because your helmet light was ahead of you on the ground being pushed along by hands that you couldn't see.

All the men had passed through like buttered pancakes leaving Tommy and me on the other side. Tommy winked at me and went through without a sound. Now on the other side, Tommy yelled to me that it was clear and I yelled back that there was no way I could do it. There was a slight pause and then Tommy's head popped back onto my side of the hole.

"What's up, Kevin? Hole got you spooked?" Tommy asked as he pulled his body out.

"That would be an understatement!" I sputtered. "I'm afraid this is where I'm going to have to draw the line, Tommy. That hole scares the wits out of me! My *cat* would have difficulty getting through that."

"Everybody else has done it, Kevin, and I know you can do this. You've been in holes this tight before."

"No, Tommy. No way," I whined.

Tommy yelled to the guys on the other side to move along and that we would catch up, and together we talked about that hole.

"Kevin, let's do this together. I'll go through and we'll discuss technique as I do. Then I'll come back again and you can try. The view from the other side is great, and you're going to love the way you feel when you get through that hole. We can do this together, just the two of us. We'll take our time. Okay?"

I muttered a halfhearted okay and off he went. In and out, lickety-split. Back again. Nothing to it.

"Now it's your turn, Kevin."

Tommy patted me on the shoulder as I took a big swallow and said a silent prayer, and then I got on my back and began the snake wiggle. I *really* did not want to go into that hole, and I could feel the panic rising in my chest as I slithered inside. Just as my head entered the hole, and seconds before I was about to call it quits, Tommy started humming the theme song to *Mission Impossible*. I slowly kept moving, and the deeper I got into that hole, the louder his humming became. Halfway into that hole I started smiling (Tommy can't carry a tune), and then I started to sing along with him. By the time we reached the best part of the song, I was on the other side, looking around at a beautiful cavern, smiling like a birthday boy at a surprise party. Tommy popped through as we finished the song, both of us humming as loud as we could. We high-fived and caught up with the crew. On the way back out, I popped through that hole like a cockroach on the way to dinner—nothing to it.

To this day when I face a challenge that really pushes me to the limit, I hum that song. It makes me smile and reminds me of Tommy Gillis and that darn hole, and it reaffirms in my mind that we are all capable of more than we think, if only we are willing to take the risk and release the Dragon Slayer inside.

Lt. Tommy Gillis and Kevin in the Whirlpool cave, having just come through the "hole from hell." Picture by Bob Parker, taken from the Kevin Baum library.

Training only serves as a tease and, in time, you want to put your skills to the real test, which is why I became interested in mountaineering. I wanted to use my skills in rope craft in an actual setting, to apply my training, and to challenge myself in ways that I had yet to experience. The 1996 disaster on Everest had piqued my interest and I wanted to see for myself what all the ballyhoo was about. So after a fair amount of research, I eventually signed up for a one-week mountaineering seminar on Mt. Rainier. I had never seen the mountain before, had never even seen a glacier, and had absolutely no idea what I was getting myself into, but I was determined to do it anyway. In May of 1997, I made my first attempt on the mountain.

After a week on that mountain, a harrowing close call with an ice avalanche, and an epic summit attempt in 70 mph winds (we turned back at 13,800 feet), I was convinced that mountaineering was the single most foolish endeavor in all of human endeavors. *These guys are nuts!* I told myself after we finally got down. My face was charred from frost-nip—the early stages of frost-bite—I had lost seventeen pounds and my body felt like it had been the kickball in a baby dinosaur's game of soccer. *Did it. Been there. Done that. Got the T-shirt. Never again*, I thought as I boarded the plane back to Texas. I didn't even look out the window as we flew by the mountain.

But somehow mountaineering had gotten into my bloodstream. Indeed, the further I got from that trip, as miserable as it was, the more I wanted to do it all over again. It's difficult to explain this feeling to people who have not shared a similar experience, but the collection of *all* the experiences I had while on Mt. Rainier was, in a strange way, cleansing. It was a back-to-the-basics, in-the-raw event that washed my soul free of all the crap that we humans tend to fill up with in our daily routines. When I think about it, climbing to me is very similar to fighting fires: when you walk away from the event, you feel a sense of renewal and a deep connection to the people that shared the experience with you. The physical act itself is not much fun and the risks are scary, but the feelings that come after are powerful and exhilarating. Risk in the pursuit of an objective, I began to believe, is healthy. It's good for the soul.

So I decided to keep at it, and I signed up for everything I could think of—ice climbing in Ouray, Colorado; avalanche rescue courses in Silverton, Colorado; wilderness medicine courses in Seattle, Washington; high-line rescue seminars in Sedona, Arizona. I slowly began to tackle smaller glaciated peaks on a variety of routes. I climbed Mt. Hood in Oregon, Mt. Shasta in northern California, Mt. Adams in Washington, and many other mountains around the country. I summited all of them, some of them several times.

But Mt. Rainier remained illusive. In fact, my efforts on Rainier were always strangely epic, as if the mountain didn't want me there, and definitely not at the top. Over the years, my attempts on Rainier resulted in two separate crevasse falls; raging snow storms that penned us in our tent for days; 100 mph winds; avalanches; and, much to my family's horror, two days in a Seattle hospital with pulmonary edema. Eventually, my family and friends began to speculate that perhaps I should leave that mountain alone. I listened to them, but kept at it anyway. I just felt so alive when I was on that mountain. How do you explain that feeling to somebody who has not been there with you?

You can't. *Everyone needs to find their own Mt. Rainier*, I mused. Trying to explain *mine* and its hold on me undermined the very power and importance of the relationship. So I just quit trying.

It was the early summer of 2002. I had just taken the promotion to assistant fire chief and I was training like a professional athlete for my sixth attempt on Mt. Rainier, scheduled for mid-July. My routine consisted of running four to eight miles a day during lunch and then hiking the greenbelt in the evenings after work. It was fun and I was enjoying the suspense of pre-climb training, as well as the constant endorphin-induced high that came along with it.

It was while I was training for Mt. Rainier that I ran into Rob Horne and his fiancée. They were out exercising together and had stopped for a drink at one of the fountains along the running trail. Rob and his wife-to-be were clearly bubbling with fresh love happiness, and their excitement about life and their future was infectious. We stood together and visited for some time. Rob was still at Station Two and he caught me up on all the latest happenings at the house; several members of the original gang were still there. I told Rob about my upcoming climb and he mentioned that he had heard I was into mountaineering. "Yeah, can't get it out of my system," I laughed. Rob mentioned that he knew how it felt, as his latest obsession was whitewater kayaking, and he had been training almost daily for the big water. His bride, an attractive redhead clearly deeply in love, looked on in admiration as we chatted.

It didn't surprise me to learn that Rob was kayaking and that he was really into it. Firefighters are always getting into some adventure or another—feeding the Dragon Slayer— and it appeared as if Rob had found his own Rainier. He was clearly running with it. *Good for him*, I thought.

We visited for a short while longer and then we shook hands and wished each other well. "See you later," I said, as we jogged off in separate directions.

Have you ever wondered what you might do differently if you could turn the clock back? I wonder that often when I reflect on that short hike and bike trail visit because that was the last time I would see Rob alive. Just before the Fourth of July, Rob would be killed in a kayaking accident on a small creek in west Austin.

It had been an extremely wet summer for Austin that year, with record rainfall during the month of June. The Highland Lakes reservoir system can only take so much runoff before the dams have to be opened and water released. All up and down the system, some reservoirs flood while others take on the torrents of raging hydraulic flows from the open dams, sending hundreds of thousands of gallons of water raging toward the Gulf of Mexico. What was once a beautiful still-water lake suitable for lazy boating can overnight become a cascading class three rapid, foaming and furious. What's more, many of the feeder creeks to the Highland Lakes system, those that dump the runoff into the river, can rage like glacier-fed mountain rapids, turning a small creek into a gulley washer overnight. To the white-water kayaker, these dangerous feeder creeks are seductive playgrounds.

It was on one of these feeder creeks where Rob met his fate. He went alone and parked his car in a surrounding neighborhood. Several skilled kayakers were already there running the rapids and then hiking back up to do it all over again. Even a local television crew was there getting video and interviews of the kayakers as they braved the torrential waters. Just before Rob put in to begin his own run, the reporter caught up to him and asked for an interview. Rob, like all firefighters, had spent a career around reporters, and the camera didn't intimidate him, so he agreed, capturing on film what is today an eerie interview of Rob's last spoken words.

"Why do you do this?" the reporter asked. "Doesn't the danger bother you?"

Rob smiled. How do you answer that question in a way that others can understand? You're asking a firefighter about danger? Rob had found his own Mt. Rainier and he was celebrating life in his own way—what looks foolish to you is not so to him. Of course there is no way to adequately answer that question; it can't be answered. So Rob said some words about being confident in his abilities, training, and so on. They were just words.

"Because it is there."

About thirty minutes later, the firefighters would find Rob in shallow water, separated from his kayak, halfway down the rapid. They pulled him out and began CPR and kept at it for a long time, but Rob had already left. He was pronounced dead on the scene.

I got the call just as I returned home from work. Rob had drowned. I was sitting in my backyard staring at my swimming pool in disbelief. *They have the identity wrong*, I thought and said as much. Rob was too smart and talented to get jammed up in a creek, and he and I had been through way too many hair-singing fires for him to go in a kayaking accident. "No, they're sure of the identity," was the sober reply.

I immediately told the caller to contact Jim Eberle. Jim and Rob had worked together for years and were close. It is department tradition (and policy) to assign a firefighter as "family liaison" when another firefighter dies; they notify the family in person of the death and then provide whatever support and help they can as the family struggles through the event. I knew it would be a tough assignment for Jim, but I couldn't think of a person more equipped for the task, and Jim had been his officer longer than anybody else in the department. He said he would call Jim immediately.

Then I went to the scene. I arrived just as they were bringing Rob up to the ambulance. The firefighters had draped an American flag over Rob's body and were treating him with amazing dignity and honor. As they loaded Rob's body into the ambulance for his final ride, everybody on scene took off their helmets and hats, stood at attention, and put their hands on their breasts. Some firefighters saluted. The only sound was the raging water in the distance. We continued to stand at attention until long after the rig drove off.

Three days later I would once again be in the company of my old Station Two pals. It was a strange reunion and the hugs and handshakes were halfhearted, but it was good to see them. The funeral home was packed with hundreds of uniformed firefighters, citizens, family members, and friends. Even the mayor was there. Almost a dozen emergency vehicles were parked on the street out front and on the side streets around the funeral home. It was an amazing turnout and a great honor to Rob. I smiled as I saw the masses of people.

As I entered the funeral home, Jim Eberle saw me over the crowd and walked up to me. We shook hands and I looked into his eyes. Jim was clearly tired, but he was strong. "How ya doing, Jim?" I asked.

"It's been a long road, Kevin, and, frankly, I'm a bit nervous about all this. I agreed to emcee the ceremony and to give a eulogy," Jim looked around. "There are a lot of people here."

I smiled at him, confident that he would be terrific. "Just be yourself Jim, and remember to breathe!" I smiled.

"Right. But I'm not going to be alone up there. Several of the guys have agreed to speak. And Kevin, I'd like you to speak, too. I know it's been a long time since you were at Station Two, but you were there with us for several years. Also, since you're now a member of the department's command staff, you can speak on behalf of the leadership. Are you up to it?" he asked.

"It would be an honor, Jim." And we went in.

The ceremony was moving and at times even fun. It was the celebration of a life more than the mourning of a death. Some of the talks were deeply sad, others just stories about Rob and his life. Occasionally they would play one of Rob's favorite songs and we would all sit back quietly and listen. Jim did a terrific job. He was deeply genuine and caring. And then he called for me to speak.

I had been wondering what I was going to say as I listened to the various speakers that day. I had heard mumblings outside about the "senselessness" of Rob's death, and I knew that his family and friends were struggling not just with the loss, but with the *way* it had happened, trying to find some sense of peace with the fact that they had lost a loved one in a kayaking accident on some nameless creek. I wanted to try to explain to this caring audience that firefighters perceive danger differently than other people; that Rob's death, while tragic, was a loud statement about his life. I couldn't piece it all together into a script before Jim called on me, so I simply took the stage and let my heart run free.

I started by telling the crowd about the honor with which the firefighters on scene had removed him—the flag, the salute, Rob's final ride. I thanked the firefighters who removed and cared for Rob that day. I then told a couple of Station Two stories, particularly the one where the rookie got stuck in the pole hole and Rob wanted to leave him there. We had a good laugh together.

And then I took a deep breath and tried to explain what Mallory could not. Here is what I said:

Lessons from the Line

"I want to talk to you for a minute about firefighters, and then I'll sit down. Firefighters are unique. I don't know if it is the job that shapes the person, or if it is the person who is attracted to the job, but firefighters tend to be different. They say that the average person will require the services of a fire department once in a lifetime, and that one event becomes the story of a lifetime for that one person. It's a *big deal* to them. But firefighters respond to events like that once-in-a-lifetime emergency of yours several times per shift. Danger is very much a part of what a firefighter does, and because of this constant exposure to danger, a firefighter tends to view it differently than most people do.

"As I look around me here today, I see firefighters that jump out of perfectly good airplanes for fun; firefighters that rappel off high-rise buildings; firefighters that scuba dive in underground rivers; firefighters that have sailed through hurricanes because they thought it would be interesting. And before you right now, you see a man who climbs mountains."

I could tell I had their attention, so I just kept pushing on.

"This is not about me; it's about Rob, but bear with me for a minute here. My family doesn't understand why I climb mountains and I can't adequately explain it to them. So, before I leave on a climb, this is what I tell my wife: 'Should I die on this trip, please understand that I died doing something that thrills my every sensibility. And please tell my mom and dad that even though they may not understand it, this is something that I feel like I have to do. Why? Because it isn't the fear of death that scares me so much. It's the fear of not living life that haunts me.

And while I certainly don't want to die, my desire to really experience *life* is stronger.'

"And I think if Rob could come here right now and say one thing to all of you, it would be something *just like that*. Because when Rob died, he died living life to its fullest. That should not only tell you something about the man, it should also tell everybody in this room a little something about successful living. And I, for one, would like to thank Rob for the reminder. So, mourn the loss of our friend and loved one, but don't mourn the way in which he went."

I shook Jim's hand and sat down.

After the ceremony, all the firefighters filed out a side door and, under Harry Evans' watchful eye (now a battalion chief), lined up in a massive Roman phalanx behind the hearse. I was on the front line. As they brought Rob's coffin out, carried by the Station Two crew, Harry screamed in his booming drill instructor's voice, "Attention!" In unison we all jumped to attention and saluted and held it while the bagpipes played "Amazing Grace."

On the long drive to the graveyard, Harry had pre-positioned fire apparatus at every exit on the highway. The rigs had been polished and were glittering in the summer sun, and the crews were standing in front dressed in their Class A's, rigidly at attention. As the convoy passed, the firefighters would salute—a final tribute to a fallen brother. Rob was buried that day and the firefighters slowly went back to work.

When Rob died, he may have died by himself, but he didn't die alone. He was never alone.

Two weeks later I was on Mt. Rainier and I was hurting. We were passing through 13,000 feet and I was hitting a wall. My climbing partner and I had been on the mountain for two days. We climbed light and fast. We didn't even take a tent. We would just dig a hole in the glacier and sleep inside, and I was feeling the effects of altitude, fatigue, and lack of sleep. I would breathe three times and kick in a crampon, breathe three times and kick in a crampon, and do it again, over and over. Every part of my psyche was screaming at me to stop and my mind was telling me that I was being stupid. The climb so far had been fairly unremarkable. We had a few close calls with falling rocks on a lower ridge and the glaciers were wildly fragmented with crevasses up high, but other than that all was well—except for me. My attitude and my body were telling me to quit and I was starting to listen.

I have discovered that the biggest challenge we will ever face in life is ourselves. Self-doubt is a festering cancer that can only be cured by experience and tenacity, and we have to be willing to face it when it shows up. But it is, nevertheless, a powerful voice of false reasoning, especially when the going gets tough. That day on the mountain, the seemingly intelligent voice in my head was telling me that mountaineering was stupid; that I was needlessly risking my life and "Hey, Kevin, you have responsibilities, you know"; that climbing is nothing but an excuse to get cheap thrills at other people's emotional expense. And I was starting to believe the voice.

As I was standing there on the mountain that day, leaning into the blasting wind, wondering what twisted arm of fate put me there, I suddenly remembered what it was that I said at Rob's funeral about living life to its fullest. If a firefighter learns anything over the course of his career, it's that every day should be a celebration of life because life can be so fleeting. I looked up at the summit and realized that it didn't really matter if I made it to the top. What mattered was the journey. Every day is a gift. It's what we do with the gift that defines us.

My climbing partner was yanking on the rope and screaming at me to get moving. I looked up and waved to him, took a deep breath, and finally slammed my axe deep into the ice and kicked in a crampon. I smiled and started humming *Mission Impossible*. "One step at a time, Kevin," I consoled myself. "And remember: you're not alone."

I *finally* got to the top of Mt. Rainier that day. As I stood on the summit, I raised my axe high and with tears in my eyes screamed at the top of my lungs, "I did it!" My partner snapped a picture at that exact moment and I carry it with me everywhere I go—a constant reminder that if we reach deep enough, we can always find that Dragon Slayer inside.

LESSON FROM THE LINE
INNOVATION & RENEWAL

"You have to risk going too far to discover just how far you can really go!"

T. S. Elliot

"It is not because things are difficult that we dare not venture. It's because we dare not venture that they are difficult."

Lucius Seneca

"Thousands of tired, nerve-shaken, over-civilized people are beginning to find out that going to the mountain is going home; that wildness is necessity; that mountain parks and reservations are useful not only as fountains of timber and irrigating rivers, but as fountains of life."

John Muir

I recently had the opportunity to work with a mid-sized city that was experiencing a frightening increase in violent crime, particularly homicides. It seemed like every time you picked up the paper or turned on the news there was another report of crime, a drive-by shooting that killed an innocent bystander, a car-jacking that led to a stabbing, or something else that was terrible. Stories like these tend to build momentum in public discourse and become, over time, self-feeding and quite disturbing. People were naturally becoming scared, wondering what was happening to their city, and they wanted some answers. As you can imagine, this issue was fiercely political and there was a healthy dose of finger-pointing going on.

I was asked to help the police department develop a set of key metrics to intelligently assess the problem and to better tell its story. But before we could get there, the police department had to admit it had a problem, and that was the difficult part. Every single officer I met with in my very short relationship with this city would readily admit that crime was on a rise, but then he would immediately tell me, in the same breath, why it was happening: "We don't have enough officers on the street."

This city, like most cities in the early twenty-first century, had been experiencing revenue shortfalls, and everybody had been tightening their belts, doing more with less. Because of the tight economy, the police department had shrunk in size and the officers were extremely bitter about it, and this bitterness was rapidly becoming a festering resentment. This resentment was revealed in a corporate mantra, and I heard it everywhere I went. "Give us more officers and crime will go down."

After hearing this so many times, I finally threw up my hands and declared, "Okay, new rule: you're not allowed to say that the problem is the number of officers on the street. The assumption, for the purposes of this conversation, is that you only get what you have already got. No more money and no more officers. Now what can we do?"

"That's a bad assumption, Kevin. We need more officers on the street."

"Okay," I would argue, trying a different approach. "What's the best way to get more officers on the street? By telling the world that crime will go down if you get more officers or by making crime go down with what you already have and demonstrating how effective you are? Think about it, which approach will 'sell' better?"

"We need more officers on the street. It's been proven time and again, more officers on the street reduce crime. That's the approach."

And that was it. Period.

My contract with that city ended as quickly as it began.

I think this story is interesting and serves as a good case study into a phenomenon that I see all too frequently in my work with organizations and the point that I would like you to consider with this chapter. Simply put, there seems to be a general risk-aversion at work in many organizations today; that is, a tendency among leaders to avoid venturing into the unknown, breaking with conventional wisdom, and really getting out of their comfort zone. In my experience, the larger the organization, the greater the tendency becomes to take refuge in the organization's very largesse and to shy away from taking great risks.

Here's the truly fascinating part: the *less* an organization supports risk-taking behavior, the *more* entrenched it appears to become in its efforts to *preserve* the status quo. This is a bizarre and very destructive cycle because the very thing that the organization needs most to reinvigorate its people, its products, and its services is the very thing it is avoiding at all costs—taking risks.

Many leaders today avoid risk and take comfort in the known in order to maintain status quo at the very time when they need to be jumping off buildings, climbing big mountains, and challenging themselves and their employees in the big waters of their work. Without risk you have no innovation. Without innovation, you have no renewal. In time, what you create is a vapid and listless organization populated with clock-watchers reciting the corporate mantra, "We need more officers on the street," or whatever it might be.

In the example of the police department, I think what was really going on was a simple case of risk-aversion—a fear of the unknown and of what it might reveal if they were to take a chance and look fear in the face. Of course it is always safer to stick with what you know and with what is comfortable. That's a given. But at what cost to you, your peers, your organization, and your customers? Do you really want to live a life absent of risk, and if so, what will that life look like? What will your organization look like?

I call this chapter the "Dragon Slayer in You" for two reasons. The first is the obvious: the dragon slayer is a metaphor for a firefighter, the man or woman who takes great risks for complete strangers by facing the dragon. Sometimes the firefighter is successful; sometimes he fails. But he always gets out there and tries. The second reason is my challenge to leaders today—to you: find the Dragon Slayer inside and let him out! Pick your Mt. Rainier, your big water, your professional or personal great goal, and go for it. Learn from the Firefighter Model and accept that risk and failure are everywhere. Stop fearing it and start celebrating it. After all, a life without risk is a life without challenge, and a life without challenge is a life of mediocrity. Is that what you want?

In the fire service, risk is a given. You can't separate the two. To avoid risk you must simply get another job. And since risk is a constant element in the firefighter's daily routine, firefighters have created a very simple motto to help them determine how and when to really put it on the line—to get way out of their comfort zone, free the Dragon Slayer, and attempt extraordinary things. Here's the motto:

> You risk a lot to save a lot.
> You risk a little to save a little.
> You risk nothing to save nothing.

So, now you know why so many firefighters and rescue personnel were killed on September 11, 2001. There was just so much to save. This simple motto helps the firefighter determine when he or she should take that great risk, the risk that can save a life or sometimes take one. On September 11, 2001, 346 firefighters and rescue personnel decided to risk a lot to save a lot, and they lost their lives in the effort.

But what incredible role models they have become for all of us, and we should learn from their example.

As September 11 taught us, we live in extraordinary times. Extraordinary times require extraordinary leaders—men and women who aren't afraid of risk, who are willing to reach deep within for the inner strength to carry them through the discomfort, uncertainty, and conflict that are ever-attendant to risk-taking—who aren't afraid to release the Dragon Slayer inside.

Indeed, in both our professional and personal lives, I am deeply convinced that we all need that Mt. Rainier out there—that big water rapid, that continuous carrot that motivates us, pushes us, challenges us, inspires those around us, and forces us to grow and improve. I am not talking about thrill-seeking. Rather, I'm suggesting a daily celebration of life. A commitment to not become a spectator to somebody else's journey, but rather an active participant in the design of your own destiny, professional or otherwise.

So, with that in mind, let's rewrite the firefighter's motto for you and your Dragon Slayer within:

> You risk a lot to gain a lot.
> You risk a little to gain a little.
> You risk nothing to gain nothing.

You decide whether or not the risk is worth taking and what you, your organization, your family, and your peers stand to gain. If you think the potential gain is a lot, then take the leap. Go through the hole. Climb the mountain. Get on the water. What are you waiting for? Remember: the hardest part about taking a risk is making the decision to do it. After that, it's just a journey. Some risks may have grave consequences, but you can live with that. After all, who among you wants to arrive safely at your death?

As you consider this question, keep in mind the words of my grandfather: *If there is no risk or controversy in your life, it's likely you aren't working on anything of consequence.*

What are *you* working on?

EPILOGUE

THE FIREFIGHTER MODEL IN REVIEW

I hope you enjoyed this short journey and found the stories and the lessons to be interesting seeds for thought and future reflection. The lessons I explore in this text aren't complicated, nor are they littered with scholarly citations. In fact, I specifically set out to write a book that was not scholastic in its approach, nor academic in its prose. Such academic texts abound and I encourage you to read them if you are of a mind.

Lessons from the Line was intended to be a personal and, I hope, engaging exploration into a few simple principles of leadership and organizational development—principles that I believe are vital in our continuing effort to create healthy organizations. And while I kept my discussion fairly narrow, you should know that there are numerous additional lessons that can be extracted from the stories I share, and I hope you will give thoughtful consideration to some of these more subtle points. In my experience, the best books for personal growth and learning are those that are indirect in their design and somewhat mysterious in their approach, forcing the reader to explore the author's deeper intent through the unique lens of his or her own personal perspective, experience, and worldview. I hope you will dig deeper to find some of these other points as you reflect on the stories and lessons I share in this short volume.

I do explore six specific principles in this book that largely define the Firefighter Model. It is important that you consider each of these lessons not as a stand-alone principle, but rather as an interdependent element in an overall synergistic leadership model—each is a piece of a mosaic rather than a snapshot. Think of the Firefighter Model as a wheel of interconnected principles, each dependent upon the other and necessary to create a powerful tool for organizational growth and development. Here's the Firefighter Model using more traditional management terms:

> Power of Purpose: Mission Clarity
> Dare to Care: Service Commitment
> Give up the Nozzle: Structured Empowerment
> Tradition Matters: Community and Fellowship
> Sleeping with Failure: Organizational Learning
> Dragon Slayer in You: Innovation and Renewal

As you reflect on this simple model, consider this:

If you have an organization that is focused on it's true purpose, harnessing the collective effort of the entire workforce toward a common and shared mission; *if* you have an organization that is populated with employees who realize that they are participants in the consumer transaction, rather than spectators, and who live this realization through a genuine commitment to customer empathy and service; *if* you have an organization that is collectively empowered to grow, challenge itself, think independently, take risks, and succeed or fail, as fate may define it; *if* your employees are connected to a deep and powerful heritage and corporate tradition that gives meaning to their work and chosen profession; *if* your workforce is allowed to learn from mistakes and to grow from the experience, rather than be punished for them; and *if* all your employees are encouraged to continuously innovate and renew themselves, your products, and your services through risk-taking and great challenge, what would you stand to gain? What would your future look like? What would the future of your organization look like? Would your people love to come to work and your customers love them for it? Would you get hugs from complete strangers?

Would you create an organization of heroes?

As you consider the Firefighter Model and how it might apply to your organization, please remember that leadership is not a function of a position within the hierarchy of an organization, but rather a human *behavior*—one that anybody can demonstrate. Many textbooks today incorrectly ascribe "leadership" responsibility to the managers and executives of organizations, as if everybody else is absolved of the responsibility to accept the leadership challenge. This is a dangerous association because in time it creates an entitlement-minded workforce that believes it is always somebody else's job to lead. They point the finger at managers and executives and cry, "Start leading!" or "We need strong leadership!" and fail to take a good hard look in the mirror. Such blame-shifting is only to avoid our own personal leadership responsibility and challenge.

I am convinced that everybody has a "firefighter" inside of them—their personal Dragon Slayer waiting to get out, to thrive, to face the fire. You should also know that I do not think that Dragon Slayers, as unique individuals, are drawn to the fire service. Rather, I think the fire service creates them. This creation, of course, is why I suggest in the title of this work that every leader should be a firefighter for a day. The trick, therefore, and the task before you, is to create a leadership synergy in your own organization where employees, managers, and executives—everybody within the enterprise—feel encouraged to dig deep and find their own personal Dragon Slayer; to create an organization where Dragon Slayers can thrive and grow, and grow your business with them. Indeed, I don't care where you are in your organization's hierarchy—front line, supervisor, manager, executive, administrative assistant—you can still lead from where you are. To do so will require great risk and discomfort, but as I hope you have learned from this short book, that's what leadership is all about.

So, here's my final challenge to you: as you accept your own leadership responsibility, ask for clarification on your true purpose; push back when you see fellow employees treat customers with dispassion and short shrift; get out of your comfort zone by trying new things, taking risks, and asking for opportunities to become empowered; celebrate the uniqueness of your company or organization, its traditions, mores, artifacts, and stories; stand up and admit when you fail, and tell the world what you learned from it and are doing about it; and finally, dare to do what you think is right, not what you think is safe.

And as you do this, take comfort in the knowledge that you are not alone. You're never alone.

Indeed, the hero is looking back at you in the mirror.

ENDNOTES

1. I fully recognize that women are firefighters too, and very good ones at that. For purely stylistic purposes, however, I have selected to use the masculine gender when referring to firefighters in this book. This is simply to reduce the clutter that comes with multiple "he or shes" littered throughout the text. I hope you understand.

2. Most fire departments refer to the initial alarm for a structure fire as a "box alarm," a term with deep roots in fire service tradition. Remember those old red fire boxes you used to see on utility poles? Those were designed for people to call in a fire when they observed one. The dispatchers would ask, "What box are you calling from?" and then send the crews to that box, which was both a communication tool and a location. Even though fire boxes are long out of use, the tradition of initiating structure fire responses with a "box alarm" designation remains to this day.

3. Rehab is an area on a fire scene where firefighters collect to rehydrate, rest, eat, and receive medical attention. Crews rotate in and out of the rehab area during a prolonged incident.

4   Obviously, most fire departments have people on staff who that are not trained as firefighters. The very power that is embedded within the shared purpose between trained firefighters can alienate those who don't share this unique perspective. To address this perceptual rift, many fire departments today are putting their non-uniform employees through a shortened "Academy," where they fight fire and learn the trade from the firefighter's perspective. This helps to bridge any perceptual gaps between sworn and non-sworn positions and reinforces the notion that "We are all in this together to save lives and property."

5   Be careful here, dear reader. Water is not the best extinguishing source for *all* fires. Some liquids have different specific gravity than water, which means they do not mix. Both grease and gasoline, for example, float on water. So, if you try to extinguish a grease fire with water, the fire essentially floats on the water, thus separating the cooling effect of the water from the fire itself. Putting water on a grease fire only makes it bigger, because you expand the surface area affected by the fire by spreading out the burning grease. Try baking soda instead (just after you dial 911!).

6   So aggressive that he threw me off the Engine one day as I was trying to board for a call; zoomed right out of the station while I hung on for dear life. I finally fell off, only to have the truck tires smash my helmet into a hundred bits as I rolled out of the way of the wheels just as they passed.

7   There is also a 6th Battalion that is functional, not regional.

8   "Standard of Coverage" is fire service lexicon and refers to the acceptable combination of firefighters, fire equipment, and fire stations necessary meet the response demands of a particular area (city, county, etc.). Standards of coverage vary, depending on the unique demands of an area (also the politics), but it is generally accepted that a fire department should be able to arrive at any location within a response area in less than eight minutes from the time the call is received, for the majority of calls.

9   The colors in this code correspond to the color of the helmet each rank wears while on the scene of a fire. Chiefs wear white helmets, captains wear red, lieutenants wear orange, and drivers and firefighters wear yellow. Since firefighters today are completely encapsulated in protective equipment when fighting fires, it is extremely difficult, if not impossible, to see who is behind the gear and the mask. We address this confusion with color-coded helmets, each with magnetic numbers that identify the rig the firefighter is riding that shift. So if a firefighter is assigned to Ladder Seventeen and gets lost in the smoke at an incident, he can simply look for the red helmet with L17 on the side and find his captain.

10 This is, of course, why today we refer to soldiers who are engaged in combat as being on the "frontline."

11 Many uninformed observers have noted that fire-

fighters frequently do as much damage as the fire. Now you know why.

12   It is for this reason that firefighters consider "first in" to be a badge of honor, and why you will see "first on scene" as a slogan or tagline for so many departments across the country.

13   Keep in mind that at a major fire you will eventually have hoses on the ground littering the area like gigantic spaghetti noodles, making it virtually impossible to move a fire apparatus from its initial placement. This is why it is so important to think before you spot your rig. Once parked, you are there for the duration. If the fire gets out of control and you didn't position your rig correctly, you just burned up a million-dollar piece of equipment.

14   A "cut-off" line is a section of two-inch hose that firefighters place on each side of the burning apartments, positioned within the structure to cut off the fire's ability to extend to unburned sections of the building. This tactic is manpower intense, but very effective if coordinated correctly.

15   A picture of these "horns" was captured for posterity by an amateur photographer. We later referred to the phenomenon as the Longhorns of the UT housing system—an epithet to the university's lackluster approach to fire safety. The university has since improved its performance in that regard.

16. Postmortem: It took several days to fully extinguish the Centennial fire and to see the full extent of the destruction, which was complete. The dollar loss for the fire was placed somewhere between 12 and 13 million. We never did find out exactly what started the second fire at the Centennial Condominiums that night. The "official" story was that a small ember had escaped our inspection earlier in the day and over the course of the afternoon had slowly increased in intensity ultimately generating enough heat to ignite surrounding combustibles. This is a good hypothesis; but, it's a hypothesis that can't be proven and one that I don't like. My peers laugh at me and tell me that the only reason I don't like this story is because I was in charge, and therefore I have to "own" the "rekindle," which is not a good thing in the fire service. I can see their point. But here's my perspective: if the fire grew slowly—which it would have *had to*, given the official story—taking *hours* to generate enough heat to ultimately involve the entire attic, penetrate the storage closets, and vent through the roof, wouldn't somebody have smelled smoke long before we got the initial call? The *entire* place was occupied that night with kids moving to and fro within and outside of the complex. Wouldn't somebody have seen something long before the fire had advanced so far? These are good questions but, unfortunately, questions that will never be answered. The fire itself destroyed all the evidence of alternate ignition scenarios and burned these secrets into

Lessons from the Line · 239

oblivion. Finally, for those readers who know about building codes and construction, you are probably wondering why the building was not sprinklered. It was. The sprinkler system didn't work. But that is another story.

17 Newton, of course, knew what he was talking about when he said that every action receives an equal and opposite reaction. If a firefighter is not prepared for the pressure blowback from opening a charged line, he will quickly find himself on his rear-end—or worse. I have seen 250-pound firefighters tossed like a horseshoe when they weren't prepared for the blowback from a pressurized hand line.

18 A "Rack" line is a 150-foot, pre-connected section of one-and-a-half-inch hose. It is called a "Rack" line because it is stored within a horizontal rack on top of a pumper and can be deployed in a matter of seconds. A skillful firefighter can quickly douse a blaze with a pre-connected "rack."

19 The name "Manpower" was a misnomer. Women rode on the Manpowers as well; we had a lot of fun back in those days 'worming' each other about the name.

20 In most fire departments, fire station numbers correspond to the order in which the buildings were built and commissioned into service. If you want to find the oldest fire station in a city, look downtown for Fire Station One and odds are you will find it.

21 Remember the days when you would see the fire-

fighters wave at you from the tailboard? Those were the good old days—and also the dangerous ones. While it was a ton of fun to be back there, if the driver went too fast or lost control on a turn, there was no telling where the two guys on the back would end up—frequently on the pavement.

22   Indeed, the tradition of fire station tours is as old as the profession itself and serves as a powerful tool to connect a department to the community it serves.

23   This really happened. I would love to give you the firefighter's name, but that would be too severe of a worm!

24   In an act illustrating their commitment to serving the community, the poor fellows bought the little girl a new pet chicken, but it "just wasn't the same."

25   This is why my entire organizational development consulting practice centers on "engaging with the workforce" before making important organizational decisions. You may be surprised by what you learn.

26   Turnover rates in the fire service are generally less than 4%.

27   There is a growing movement in the United States to incorporate residential sprinklers into new construction of single- and multi-family homes. The data is in and indisputable that residential sprinklers dramatically improve your chances of surviving a home fire. However, to date, most efforts to get residential sprinklers into local legislation have been soundly

defeated by the construction and apartment association lobbies.

28 So, next time a city or county official requires you to pull a permit for a new addition or building, rather than complaining, try saying, "Thanks!"

29 Two of the boys were brothers and the third was a visiting friend.

30 A quick word about fire fatality statistics: For national reporting purposes, any fatality where fire is the proximate cause of the death is recorded as a fire fatality, whether the death is in a structure or not. For example, if a person is involved in a vehicle accident, survives the impact, but is subsequently killed by a resultant fire, it is recorded as a fire fatality. Not all of the twenty-four fatalities recorded in the eighteen-month period occurred in the home. Regardless, no matter how you slice the data, the numbers were staggering, and of the fires that did occur in the home, they occurred in the absence of a working smoke alarm.

31 This is a mystery to us. Did she see the Freddy message in the media and test the alarm, only to discover it wasn't working and leave it to fix for another day? Or was the smoke alarm disassembled prior to hearing the Freddy message? Did she see the door hanger that night before she died, and if so, why didn't she fix the alarm? Unfortunately, these are questions we'll never be able to answer.

32 If any other city the size of Austin can make the same claim, I have yet to find it.

33 A young boy was playing with fire by a Christmas tree. The tree caught fire and since he was home unsupervised, he hid from the fire in the closet and perished there. The smoke alarm worked.

34 The Hurricane Katrina debacle comes to mind here.

35 Mallory died in 1924 attempting to summit Everest. His body was found in 1999, seventy-five years later. The location of his body caused a wave of speculation that he may have actually topped the mountain before he perished, potentially stealing the honor of first summit from Sir Edmund Hilary, who stood atop the mountain in 1953.

36 Mechanical advantage is created whenever you have a moving pulley within a rope system. In the simplest terms, a moving pulley reduces the load that you have to pull in order to lift or move a heavy object, such as a patient stuck in a hole. For example, if you have a two-to-one mechanical advantage and you are trying to lift a 200-pound patient, your load at the haul line is only 100 pounds. If you have a four-to-one mechanical advantage system, you now only have fifty pounds of load at the haul line. If rigged correctly, a single firefighter can lift a 200-pound patient with only one arm.

ACKNOWLEDGMENTS

Lessons from the Line has been a labor of love, but labor nonetheless. To those who have helped me carry the burden, I thank you. Thank you to my wife, Gwen, for her support and encouragement and to my friends and clients all over the world who said, "I'd read that book, Kevin!" To my readers for their insight and wisdom—Will Godwin, Robbie Aldman, Mike Conlin, James Kiberd, Gail Baum, Brian French, and Kelley Sutherland—I can't thank you enough. To my mom and dad for their inspiration, and to my grandfather who is beside me always, I thank you all.

Finally, to the men and women of the Austin Fire Department and the fire services everywhere, may *Lessons from the Line* please you and serve as a source of pride as you move forward in your own personal leadership journey.

Godspeed.

AUTHOR'S NOTE

Winston Churchill used to say that history would smile upon him because he intended to write it. With this statement, I don't think Churchill was suggesting that he intended to rewrite history or that he was going to falsely portray the events that made up his personal story. Rather, I think he was simply recognizing that it was impossible to separate historical events from his own perspective of those events.

I would say the same to you as you read *Lessons from the Line*. The stories I share in this short book are true, but my perspective of them is inextricably woven into the very tapestry of my own involvement in them. I quite naturally have my own opinion of the stories and their consequences, and I suppose it is possible that others might have different takes on the conclusions I draw from them. The Freddy Finger story provides the perfect example of this potential discord. Freddy Finger was a creative and novel approach to a long-standing public safety problem, and eighteen months after his introduction, the City of Austin was still free of fatal fires. When I retired twenty-two months after Freddy hit the streets, the city had experienced only one fire fatality and a working smoke alarm wouldn't have made a difference in that fire's outcome. There have been some that would make the argument that the sudden and dramatic drop in fatal fires was a lark, a fluke, and not related to the Freddy Finger campaign at all. Even though it is unlikely that Freddy was completely responsible for the amazing turnaround in fire fatalities, to deny his causal role in the turnaround at all is to simply deny statistical reasoning. Regardless, as the Freddy story illustrates, the opinions and perspectives I present in this book are all my own, and I accept that others may have divergent interpretations.

You should also know that I took some literary license with this book. Many of the stories I share are somewhat anachronistic—events taken out of time and in some cases out of context—in order to create a readable and engaging text. It would have been ridiculously pedantic to keep each story within its true timeframe and chronology, in my opinion, and the reader would have quickly become lost in the tedium of microscopic accuracy. Thus, I took some liberties in order to keep the stories moving.

I also relate a number of conversations in this book. These conversations are as close to accurate as a forty-five-year-old mind can make them, recognizing that I have slept a few nights since they occurred. In those cases where my memory failed me the exact words, I tried to make the tone and content of the conversations accurately reflect the personalities as I know them and the events as I remember them. Did Harry Evans really say, "This is our Alamo"? I don't know; but I can tell you that he said something to that effect, and I can definitely see Harry saying those exact words under similar circumstances.

Some of the names in this book are real, others are not. If I made up a name, it was to protect the individual's privacy. If I used a real name, I did so out of complete respect for the actual person, as I wanted him to know how I truly feel about him and the role he has played in my career and life. To those people who see their actual names in this book (and to their family and friends), know that I have nothing but respect for you, and I apologize if my description of you is less than perfect. Please accept that my effort was made with perfect intentions.

ABOUT THE AUTHOR

Author Kevin Baum is the former assistant fire chief and fire marshal with the Austin, Texas, Fire Department, and is the founder and president of inCentergy, an Austin-based organizational and leadership development consulting group. Kevin's ideas on leadership and performance have been published in journals in the United States, Canada, the United Kingdom, Australia, and South Africa. His research into organizational conflict and group dynamics was recognized by the National Association of Schools of Public Affairs and Administration as Best in America in 1997. Kevin is a popular motivational speaker and consultant with clients from around the world. He has a BA from Western Illinois University and a master's of public policy and administration from Texas State University.

For more information on Kevin Baum or the inCentergy Consulting Group, visit www.inCentergy.com or www.PerformanceSherpa.com. Kevin can be reached at KBaum@inCentergy.com.